PROUDER THAN EVER

Major A.T. Casdagli, RAOC.

PROUDER THAN EVER

My War + My Diary + My Embroideries

A.T. CASDAGLI

compiled by
ALEXIS PENNY CASDAGLI

CYLIX PRESS

LONDON
www.cylixpress.co.uk

Cylix Press would like to express grateful thanks to G . F Smith, the Purepint Group,
Gravity Matrix, Studio 22, Hain Daniels and John Ross for their support.

Design and Layout: Chris R. McDermott
Cover design and Image Development: Phil Irish

Typeset by Studio 22, London
Printed in England by the Pureprint Group on paper from a sustainable source

ISBN: 978-0-9926759-6-7

April 2015

for Chis Tolman,

my father was such a proud Grovite and would be so overwhelmed by the terrific honour the school are paying him in the wonderful exhibition at the OSRG — and all our family —

For my father and mother

kind regards.

Alexis Perry

CONTENTS

INTRODUCTION

This diary was kept in Germany during the Second World War in the various prisoner of war camps in which my father, Major A. T. Casdagli, was incarcerated, despite the risk of confiscation or reprisals. It has not been censored by the German authorities. For security reasons, little or no mention is made of escapes or methods or preparation for escapes. Similarly, no mention is made of other subversive activities which formed such an important part of prison life.

This diary was always kept carefully hidden as prisoner of war camps were subject to endless searches. Apart from the daily, routine searching of rooms, kit and men, the diary records twenty-seven instances of major searches. Of these, six were carried out by the Army and civilians and two by the Gestapo. The Gestapo were the secret police force of the Nazi Party empowered to torture prisoners, send people to concentration camps and carry out many other ruthless acts in the name of protecting the German state. On one of these two occasions, forty Gestapo agents searched the camp, Oflag XII-B, for four hours while the prisoners were kept in the yards. Yet, in spite of all this, remarkably, the diary was never discovered.

In compiling the diary for publication, short extracts from my father's letters have been included in diary entries of the same date, as well as several pieces of writing from his War Log. This small book was given to prisoners of war (POWs) by the Young Men's Christian Association (YMCA), for them to record what they were thinking and doing during their captivity.

The diary seems to fall naturally into parts and chapters. Almost all take their title from a word or a phrase in the chapter or part they name. The text is illustrated with photographs, letters, newspaper cuttings, maps and other documents. All, unless otherwise stated, were carefully collected by my father at the time and found amongst his papers after his death. Endnotes have been provided, which I hope will be useful, giving facts and background information about people and events referred or alluded to in the diary.

Spelling has been modernised; for instance, 'to-day' becomes 'today'. Occasionally, additional paragraphs and punctuation have been introduced for clarity and the rare missing word has been replaced but, beyond that, only minor editing of the text was necessary.

Distances are in miles, yards, feet and inches (one mile equalling 1.6 kilometres), although the dimensions the embroideries and other art works are in millimetres for greater accuracy. Temperatures are in Fahrenheit. Weights

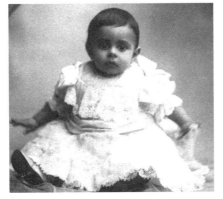

December 1906.

Christening, 1907.

Kersal Hill, Salford.

Villa Casdagli, Cairo, Egypt.

are in pounds and ounces, one pound (1 lb) being 0.40 of a kilogram. Sterling is calculated in pounds, shillings and pence: one pound has twenty shillings and one shilling is equal to two sixpences or twelve pence.

My father was born on 10 April 1906 in Salford, a cotton town in the metropolitan borough of Greater Manchester in North West England. He was an anglicised Greek and, like his father and grandfather, his nationality was British.

He was christened Alexis Theodore but no one ever called him Alexis. Rather, he was always Lecky, Leck, Cas or simply Casdagli, (pronounced: kaz'dag'lee). The name originates in Turkey, Casdagli being the anglicised form of Kazdagli, meaning 'from the Kazdagi Mountain'. The Kazdagi Mountain, or 'Goose' Mountain, is in the Balikesir Province of northwest Turkey. It is the sacred Mount Ida of ancient times and the ruins of Troy lie about 20 miles to its southeast.

His father, Theodore Emmanuel Casdagli, was a merchant who, with his brothers Demetrius and Xenophon, ran Emmanuel Casdagli & Sons, the shipping business their father, a naturalised Russian Greek, founded in 1860. Specialising in cotton and woollen goods, the business operated in Manchester and in Cairo, Egypt, where they had a magnificent house called the Villa Casdagli.

On 28 January 1898, Theodore, who was also the Greek Consul in Manchester, married Catherine Ralli of the Greek merchant trading family whose company, Ralli Brothers, operated internationally. They lived in Kersal Hill, 22 Singleton Road, in Kersal, Salford. Casdagli was their second son. Emmanuel was the oldest. His sister Maria, always called Menda, a lone twin, came third. The youngest was Theodore, also known as Tiny.

The children were educated at home by a governess, Miss Allen, and various tutors for languages, mathematics and music. Casdagli didn't speak until he was two. His first words were: 'You're missing a button, Mother.'

In May 1914, Casdagli went south to a boarding school 200 hundred miles away. Stanmore Park Preparatory School was a 'prep' school for Harrow and Eton Schools and had a great tradition of playing cricket. Emmanuel was already there and Casdagli, who was already passionate about cricket, was looking forward to going The headmaster, the Rev. Vernon Royle, also from Lancashire, was a first-class cricketer and a brilliant fielder who played for Lancashire and England. Legend has it that on one occasion he was so fast he caught a swallow in full flight instead of the ball.

Two and half months later, on 28 July, the First World War broke out and lasted until 11 November 1918.

In January 1920, Casdagli went to Harrow School, a large independent

Battleship, A. T. Casdagli, 1912.
Watercolour. 125 x 250 mm

Stanmore Park
Preparatory School, 1914.

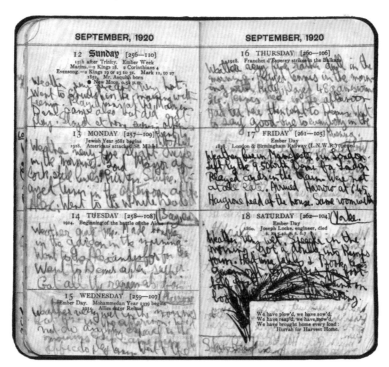

Diary, 12 – 18 September 1920.

boarding school founded in 1572, just four miles from Stanmore Park Preparatory School. He joined his elder brother Emmanuel at The Grove, one of its twelve boarding houses. At The Grove was a boy several years his senior called Frank Harold Hargrove. Hargrove was a brilliant student and excellent cricketer. He was also a School Monitor, a boy with authority over other boys, like a prefect, and Casdagli admired him greatly.

In his first year at Harrow, Casdagli kept a diary. He was not to keep another for over 20 years. His entry for Friday, 17 September 1920 reads:

'Weather fine in Manchester. Wet in London. Left by 9.50 with Demi for London. Played cards on the train. Were not at all late. Arrived at Harrow at 6.45. Hargrove head of the house [sic]. In same room with Yorke.'

Casdagli, who hated playing cards, was travelling with his uncle Demetrius, Demi for short. The 'Head of House' is chosen by the School to be the senior of all boys in the House, including any Monitors, and is a great honour.

Casdagli excelled at Harrow. Amongst other achievements, he won cups for running and prizes for boxing; was the Champion School Fencer; editor of The Harrovian and elected to the Philathletic Club, made up of the School's top athletes, and to its committee. He played squash, a game almost certainly invented at Harrow School and officially founded as a sport in its own right in 1864. He was in the School and House Eleven for cricket and for football. In 1924, Casdagli was made a Monitor and Head of House himself. On 18 September 1924, Hargrove wrote, 'My dear Cas, Just a line to wish you best of all luck as Head of The Grove. I hope you thoroughly enjoy the position and get away with as little trouble as possible'.

Casdagli also had other heroes. One was Al Kenny, the 'Salford Dreadnought', a professional welterweight boxer who taught him boxing in the school holidays. Another was T. E. Lawrence or Lawrence of Arabia, the British Army officer who led the Arab Revolt of 1916-1918 against the rule of the Ottoman Empire.

After his schooling, Casdagli, like his eldest brother, joined the family business, Emmanuel Casdagli & Sons, although he would have liked to have gone to university and become an archaeologist.

In the winter of 1930 he fell in love with Joyce E Ross Lowe. It was a whirlwind romance. They got engaged in the spring of the following year. On 18 April 1931, he wrote to his cousin, Dorothea,

"As you can imagine Joyce and I are quite up in the air about it all and very, very happy and only waiting now to 'clinch the deal'. It will be amusing to you I dare say to read of this engagement as you saw the whole thing develop. The Evening News gave the headline 'Cricketer to Wed' and then underneath 'A. T. Casdagli engaged to Miss J. E. Ross Lowe' and then a sort of account!

Harrow School Football XI *versus* Old Grovites, 1923.
Casdagli cross-legged left. Hargrove front row centre right.

Monitor and Head of House, The Grove, 1924.

Cover for T.E. Lawrence's *Revolt in the Desert*.
Brocade, silk and carving.

Al Kenny,
the 'Salford Dreadnought'.

Wedding Day, London, 9 July 1931.

Amateur Squash Champion of Egypt,
Bonne Egyptienne, 4 January 1937.

Squash Players. 195 x 165 mm

Quite a good advertisement. I was in London this week and now am just waiting until I can hit the trail once more. It's a grand life and Father, Mother and everyone have been very, very kind."

Joyce and Casdagli were married in the Holy Trinity Brompton Church, London less than three months later. Their son, Anthony, known as Tony, was born 12 June 1932. They soon moved into their own house in Knutsford, fifteen miles south of Kersal Hill.

In 1934, Casdagli left England with his wife and baby son to run two cotton farms which Emmanuel Casdagli & Sons had acquired in Egypt. They lived in the Villa Casdagli with other family members. Also living with them was an inventor whose patron was Casdagli's father. He spent his days in the basement of the Villa, which had fifteen rooms, trying to discover the secret of perpetual motion on a contraption made of bicycle wheels.

Casdagli continued playing squash in Egypt and in 1937, he became Amateur Squash Champion of Egypt beating his opponent, H. D. Nicholson in straight sets. For this he was made an Old Harrovian of Distinction. In 1939, he was runner up in the Ryder Cup Squash Rackets held at the Gezira Sporting Club in Cairo. At about this time, he also started to embroider, a very unusual activity for a man. His first piece in cross-stitch was of two squash players.

On 1 September 1939, Germany invaded Poland. Great Britain declared war on Germany two days later. On 23 September 1939, Casdagli reported to the Head Quarters for British Troops in Egypt which was in Cairo where he was commissioned as a Lieutenant into the Royal Army Ordnance Corps. The RAOC was a supply and repair corps, responsible for the repair of all army equipment and vehicles as well as for supplying weapons, armored vehicles and other military equipment, ammunition and clothing. It was also in charge of laundry, mobile baths and photography.

On 25 September 1939, Casdagli said goodbye to his wife and family and was posted to the Abbassia Depot on the outskirts of Cairo, about six miles away from the Villa Casdagli. On 6 April 1940, Casdagli went to the Sarafand Depot in Palestine as Ordnance Officer and was promoted to Captain. On 2 November of that year, he was sent to the Greek island of Crete as Deputy Assistant Director of Ordnance to Services (D.A.D.O.S). On 9 May 1941 he was promoted to the rank of Major.

And it is in Crete, sixteen days later that this diary begins.

War Log with *Embroidered Band*. 170 x 120 mm

CAPTURE

Der vom „Cormoran" versenkte australische Kreuzer „Sydney" (6830 t)   Aufnahmen: Archiv Grüner

HMAS *Sydney.* Unknown German newspaper.

*Immediately on the outbreak of war between Greece and Italy, British
troops are rushed to Crete.*

Arriving in Crete, *Picture Parade*, 23 November 1940.

1. LAST DAYS OF FREEDOM

The affair starts in May 1941 on the Greek island of Crete during the last few days fighting before the Battle of Crete[1] was lost and the evacuation of the Allied orces was attempted – I say 'attempted' because for many of us it was an attempt which failed.

I had been stationed on Crete since 5th November 1940 when we landed from HMAS 'Sydney'[2] a few days after Metaxas's 'OXI'.[3] We were met on the quay by the German Consul! As the DADOS, I was the officer in charge of all Ordnance Stores for the garrison. I had my headquarters and billet at the Agrokipion, which in peacetime is the Agricultural Experimental Station. It had originally been Brigade Headquarters and lies almost half-way between Chania and Suda Bay, rather nearer to the latter on the northwest coast of the island.

Well, there we were, being bombed literally from sunrise to sunset. The Germans had landed parachute troops on 20th May and since then the battle had been on. Our own particular contact with the enemy had been intense bombing and machine-gunning from the air. As the prelude to the dropping of the parachute troops had been a 'blitz'[4] on our anti-aircraft position, we had little resistance to offer the German aeroplanes which had everything their own way.

I was in my office at dusk on 25th May 1941, when a British sergeant brought in a civilian, whom he had found in the foothills and who was suspected of being up to no good, as he had no papers of any sort and the language difficulty had prevented any explanation being made.

Being able to speak Greek, it was natural that in those awkward days, when daylight movement was difficult, if not impossible, owing to the enemy aircraft, that any questioning of civilians or suspected characters found in the neighbourhood should be done by me. In many cases I was able to identify perfectly innocent villagers, who had come into Chania to buy what few necessities were still available and who had been held up by a patrol on their way back to their village in the evening, when the enemy planes had gone. Our patrols were strict and any person found wandering about was stopped and interrogated, for parachute troops had already been dropped by the Germans and wild rumours were the order of the day.

The man, a tough-looking customer, appeared delighted to find someone to whom he could speak in his native tongue and rapidly began to unburden himself of his story, which was briefly as follows.

He was a murderer! He had been sentenced to fifteen years' imprisonment

German parachutists, Crete. Unknown magazine, 1941.

and had completed about half his sentence. His wife and children, whom he had not seen for over seven years, were in Chania. I was watching him pretty closely and noticed that under his rough jacket and trousers he still wore the broad blue and yellow stripes of the Cretan convict.

The first parachute troops dropped by the Germans[5] had landed in the grounds of the civil gaol out towards Galatas, five miles west from here. They had quickly taken possession of the buildings and had shot the governor and the wardens. Next, they had released the convicts, only to employ them themselves as porters for their equipment. In small parties, they were marched off at the point of a tommy gun, carrying parachute containers and other equipment for the Germans. My murderer, whose name unfortunately I forget, was one of a party of three convicts, who were detailed to carry equipment under escort away from the prison grounds.

After about half an hour's journey, which with the heavy loads they were carrying may have been anything up to a mile or more, they were told to dump the loads. The containers were opened and the Germans proceeded to erect a wireless station, complete with collapsible mast. In a very short time the station was operating. The murderer then proceeded to explain to me in minute detail exactly where this station had been erected: so accurately did he describe the surroundings that I immediately passed on the information to Force Headquarters, but whether any subsequent action was taken, I do not know.

Having completed the erection of the station and mast, the murderer, knowing the countryside well, decided to make a bolt for it and, although shot at, made good his getaway into the friendly olive groves. The Germans did not trouble to follow him, thinking no doubt that one escaped convict more or less was of no vital importance. From the olive groves, the murderer made for the hills and attempted to put as great a distance as possible between himself and the Germans, as quickly as he could.

Eventually he arrived at the village of Theriso, where the King of Greece, who had come to Crete after the collapse on the mainland, was reputed to be.[6] The murderer was told that the King was there waiting for the chance to get away to Egypt. This he managed to do, by what means I do not know, but the story has it that a Sunderland flying boat flew him and his entourage to Egypt.[7]

By this time I was perfectly satisfied with the man's story and accordingly told the sergeant of the patrol that he could leave the man in my charge, and that I was satisfied that he was not a German in disguise, or a fifth columnist.[8] The fact that he was a murderer seemed unimportant! At Theriso, the murderer obtained a coat and a pair of trousers to cover his prison uniform and was attempting to make his way back to Chania to find his wife and children, whom he had not seen for so long, when he was picked up by the British patrol.

He was greatly relieved to see the sergeant go and begged that he also might be allowed to go to his home that night, saying that he would come back next morning and report to me again. I could see he was famished and sent him to the cookhouse for a meal. The troops by now had discovered that he was an escaped murderer and he was the object of much curiosity while he ate his bully[9] and drank his tea. His only desire, however, was to be off home and he did not linger long over his meal. There was something about his tough face that seemed honest – I never doubted his story for a moment. Only with difficulty could we persuade him to take a couple of tins of bully with him. He was profuse in his thanks when I told him he was free to go, and I thought I had seen the last of him.

Next morning at 9.00 am when the German planes were already busy, he turned up again, and, still expressing his great gratitude, placed himself at my disposal. He had found his family who were overjoyed to see him. I told him the best thing he could do was to go back to them as the next few days were not likely to be very comfortable.

Before going, he gave me full particulars about the German paratroops which he had seen, describing their equipment, containers, weapons, etc. At that time there were not many people who had been in close contact with this new type of soldier and his information was most useful. Murderer or no murderer, he certainly was a most observant man, for none of the details which he gave proved to be, in any way, inaccurate.

Next he told me about his own trouble, which had resulted from a row in a café. He had been insulted one night when he himself had taken enough drink to have lost his sense of proportion, and this ended in the drawing of his knife and the man who had insulted him was stabbed to death. At last, after renewed thanks and mutual wishes of good luck, the murderer left. Somehow we had all taken a liking to him and could share his joy at the reunion with his wife and children.

I often wonder what happened to him. Did the long arm of the law again lay its hand on him to complete his sentence? Was he killed in the next few days bombing and fighting? Or did he manage to get away up into the hills with his family?

Later that day, I was sent for by Lt Col. Rooke, who had come from the mainland and taken over the duties of Senior Ordnance Officer. Force Headquarters had withdrawn from Chania to Kalibes about ten miles east of Suda Bay. I went in company with Richards, one of my officers, and I was told that ALL the Ordnance personnel on the island were to be evacuated to Egypt and were to proceed to Kalibes at once – EXCEPT myself, Richards and Frost, making three officers and twenty men.

We, the unlucky ones, were to be kept on the island to form and administer an 'Ordnance Dump' of stores expected to arrive by warship from Egypt, as all our existing stores had been destroyed in Chania or were in the process of being destroyed by bombing in the sheds around the Agrokipion. When I asked where this dump was to be, I was told at the Agrokipion! I protested and said this was sheer madness as our position was known from the air and, moreover, due to the intense bombing of Suda Bay, it would be impossible to handle stores there.

Eventually Lt Col. Rooke, after interviews with 'higher authority', came round to my way of thinking and it was decided to evacuate the Agrokipion and start a new dump near the village of Stylos, about ten miles south of Kalibes. The dump would be in an olive grove and would be camouflaged as well as possible. The result of this decision was that Richards remained behind with Rooke and was to meet me at dawn next morning on the Suda-Kalibes road where the road forks south for Stylos. All the other Ordnance personnel were on their way (as they thought) to Egypt and I returned in my Austin van to the Agrokipion as fast as possible.

Frost and I got the twenty men together. The remainder went off with Roger Elletson and I saw them no more – at least not until we were all virtually prisoners. The Agrokipion had to be hurriedly evacuated; we destroyed what important documents we could find, loaded up my Austin and an 8-cwt truck with our few personal belongings, the men's kit and as much food as we could take, and set them off for Stylos.

At about 1.00 am Frost and myself and our small party started our march to Stylos. The road by this time was a thick stream of troops going the same way as ourselves – Australians, New Zealanders, all sorts of mixed British units – all of them with stories that the Germans were 'just up the road'. Only with great difficulty did we manage to keep them together. Through the night we marched and at dawn met Richards as arranged. From the fork in the road we had another trudge to the site of the new dump. Having arrived there, we tried to take stock of the situation. Here we were to start the new Ordnance dump – no stores, no telephone, no tents, no paper, no communications – NOTHING. Moreover, as 27th May progressed from dawn to morning, the position began to look worse: the stream of retreating troops still came flowing back and what shook me was the fact that the stream was now flowing right through the new dump – that is the dump-that-was-to-be!

At about 9.00 am I recognised a face in the stream. This proved to be Warrant Officer Mitchell, of the RAOC, who had been attached to the Marines. I asked him the position to which he answered,

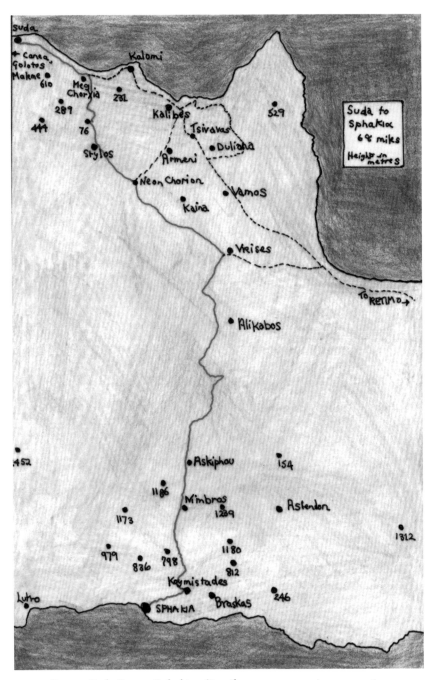

Route, Suda Bay to Sphakia, 62 miles over mountainous terrain.

'We're evacuating – haven't you been told, sir? Here's the order.'

I read the order and true enough the order was for all troops to evacuate, as best they could, to the village of Sphakia, where the necessary arrangements had been made for transport to Egypt! Here was a pretty kettle of fish. Fortunately, we had a despatch rider with us and before sending him to where I thought Force HQ were, I managed to 'appropriate' a 3-ton lorry and enough petrol for Sphakia.

Being able to speak Greek, I had arranged with a civilian and his wife to come with us as guides – I had been once, in happier days, to Sphakia but I did not know the road from Stylos. Having made all arrangements, I sent the despatch rider to Rooke with a note telling him that I had seen the evacuation order, that I had made all arrangements for my party to get to Sphakia, that I proposed to leave just before dusk and that I held myself responsible for the safety of the men.

Shortly after noon, the despatch rider returned, bringing a few thousand drachmas[10] from Rooke and also a note telling me that I came under his orders, and that I was not to move without his instructions. Moreover, he required the despatch rider at HQ and I must send him there. So there was the position quite clear. We were evacuating, but I had to await orders from Rooke before moving.

The day wore on. Ominous reconnaissance planes had been over the grove, which was now like an armed camp with lorries, mostly abandoned, some loaded with ammunition, stores, etc., and the never-ending steam of straggling troops making south. I remember I opened a tin of plums with a pickaxe and devoured the lot!

In the afternoon I spent the time digging a trench under a tree – just in case – little knowing that shallow though it was – it certainly saved my life, or at any rate saved me from injury. Sure enough, at about 3.00 pm over came the bombers and the fighters attracted by the stream of troops and masses of vehicles. Then began three quarters of an hour of hell let loose. That grove was pasted with everything they had. When their bombs were finished, they emptied their machine guns and then the real trouble started. Many lorries caught fire, including at least three loaded with ammunition. Soon the place was an inferno – I, in my trench, was better off than most. Previously, I had told the men to spend the time as they liked, not to move without my orders and to take cover and keep out of sight. Eventually the planes went away well pleased, I should imagine, with their damage done.

We then reviewed the situation. The ammunition was still going off spasmodically from the burning and burnt out lorries; our own lorry, in which we hoped to get away, was safe. None of my men were wounded but

Sphakia being bombed. Unknown newspaper.

several others were wounded and some killed.

Dusk came and went but still no word from Rooke. At 9.00 pm there was still no news. I then called Frost and Richards and explained the position and told them I was going to disobey orders and leave. They backed me up.

The stream continued. It is doubtful if any message was ever sent from Rooke. It certainly never reached me. In that pandemonium, increased by darkness, it was quite impossible to make any contact at all. So we set off.

We had not gone many miles before further progress was impossible and, moreover, there were 'walking wounded' on the road. Our lorry was by now, about 11.00 pm, a crawling mass of men hanging on, on the roof, everywhere. At last, at one block I decided to abandon it to the RAMC. One vehicle of theirs had broken down with wounded on board.

By this time I was on the road I knew and I explained to the men that we were going to reach Sphakia on foot – I did NOT tell them it was the best part of forty miles over very hilly country. I impressed on them the necessity of sticking together and not straggling. Frost went ahead and Richards and I behind. By now, the stream had thinned but I knew we could not reach Sphakia without lying up all day, as the evacuation order had stressed that no movement was to be made in daylight. I reckoned we could get to the plain of Askifou and there lie up for the day of 28th and proceed again that night and make Sphakia.

We certainly made good progress but it needed a lot of coaxing to encourage the men on the last few stretches. We rested five minutes in every half hour. Frost and Richards are not young men but they stuck it alright. Fortunately I was very fit, as it meant going up and down the line (we marched in single file) and carrying the men's kits and rifles in turn.

At dawn we made the plain and I told the men to scatter, to keep under cover, sleep and rest all day and meet again at a given spot at 7.00 pm. We had taken what food we could each of us carry. We passed a moderately comfortable day – my mind was in too much of a turmoil for sleep – and we all imagined that we were bound for Egypt and this kept the men going. The order about movement by day was NOT observed by others and troops came straggling in all day. A few German planes were over but no bombing. One plane machine-gunned up and down several times.

We met at 7.00 pm and started our march again. We reached Nimbros, the last village before Sphakia, where we met masses of troops, and an even worse pandemonium than before. It was here we got separated. Eventually Richards and I were left alone, after we had decided to abandon making Sphakia that night, as rumours had come back that the village had been bombed. There was no cover and no troops must proceed further as the road was jammed.

COPY OF CAPITULATION ORDER.

FROM :- MAJOR GENERAL. WESTON.
TO :- LIEUT-COLONEL COLVIN.

IN VIEW OF THE FOLLOWING FACTS :-

A. MY ORDERS DIRECT ME TO GIVE PREFERENCE IN
EVACUATION TO FIGHTING TROOPS, THIS HAS
REDUCED THE ACTIVE GARRISON BELOW WHAT
IS NECESSARY FOR RESISTANCE.

B. NO RATIONS WERE LEFT THIS SATURDAY NIGHT,
MOST OF THE TROOPS ARE TOO WEAK OWING TO
SHORTAGE OF FOOD AND HEAVY STRAIN TO ORGANISE
FURTHER RESISTANCE.

C. THE WIRELESS WILL GIVE OUT IN A FEW HOURS AND
THE RISK OF WAITING FOR INSTRUCTIONS FROM MIDEAST
CANNOT BE ACCEPTED AS THIS WILL LEAVE THE OFFICER IN
CHARGE WITHOUT ANY GUIDANCE AS TO HIS COURSE
OF ACTION

D. THERE IS NO FURTHER POSSIBILITY OF EVACUATION.

I THEREFORE DIRECT YOU TO CONTACT SUCH SENIOR OFFICERS AS
ARE AVAILABLE IN THE EARLY HOURS TO-MORROW AND TRANSMIT
THESE ORDERS TO THE SENIOR OF THEM.
THESE ORDERS DIRECT THIS OFFICER TO MAKE CONTACT WITH
THE ENEMY AND TO CAPITULATE.   Signed :- Weston
    SPHAKIA . 31/5/41.   Maj. Gen.

Capitulation Order, 31 May 1941.

So Richards and I, now alone, spent the day of 29th May in a ravine waiting for darkness. By now any chance of keeping the men together had gone – I imagined Frost was with some of them. In any case, I had told them 'make for Sphakia' – there we hoped we should find order and organisation. We spent an uneventful day; the two of us made the outskirts of Sphakia that night, but without any chance of getting anywhere near the beaches. We found a cave in the rocks in which we rested till the afternoon. We then set out for the village to try and find out what arrangements were being made.

Here again we found pandemonium. We also found some of our men and gradually collected them all together. We also found others from the RAOC who had originally gone to Kalibes and had from there done the same march as ourselves.

By now we were getting hungry and there were only rumours of rations having been left by the evacuating ships. Richards and I later in the afternoon walked to Kommistades where there were masses more men waiting to be evacuated. Kommistades is about five miles west of Sphakia. There we found more RAOCs who joined us.

There were rumours that men had to march in parties of fifty to the beaches at nightfall. We were then near enough to fifty ourselves, so waited till dark outside Sphakia, which had again been bombed.

It was obviously not going to be a picnic.

That night it was again impossible to get to the beaches; the village had been picketed by our troops and only 'priority' parties were allowed through. We saw the Maori Battalion[11] on their way and, knowing what fine work they had done, we didn't grudge them their luck. As the night wore on, it became more and more certain that it would be 'next night' – that is 31st May. Richards and I and our now-collected men spent an uncomfortable and hungry night on the rocks.

Next day the food question became urgent. In the afternoon I located Force Headquarters in a cave. All this afternoon mortar and machine-gun fire were clearly audible, which did not sound encouraging. I was told at Force HQ that there were no rations to be had – some were expected that night. At 9.30 pm I was told there was no chance of embarkation for Egypt – only a reduced number of ships had come and all space was booked. If I reported to HQ next morning at 10.00 am they would know if rations had come and would sign my chit. I returned to our cave by the seashore where we had gone to – Richards, I and about forty men.

Next morning at 9.00 am I set out with another man (I forget his name) to Force HQ. There were many planes overhead coming down low to machine-gun any moving object – we had to be careful. I had not gone

Kreta gefangene Briten werden abgeführt. Sie haben der überlegenen Gefechtsführur der deutschen Fallschirmjäger und Luftlandetruppen nicht standhalten können
Aufn. PK-Jesse-Scher

Allied troops surrendering, Crete. Casdagli, left.
Unknown German newspaper. Caption translates: 'The British on Crete are led away. They could not hold out against the superior fighting of the German paratroops and airborne landing commandos.'

far by 9.30 am when I heard a new noise. A bang – then a whistling – then an explosion BEHIND US! There was only one solution: the Germans had arrived at the cave where Force HQ had been and were now firing mortars from there, which were bursting somewhere near where our own cave was. Any attempt to go further would have been useless. We retraced our steps, now having the added hazard of the mortars, but the whistling gave one due warning.

I arrived at the cave and broke the news to the others. We decided to wait a while and see what happened. Meanwhile we posted a lookout to keep watch on the hill on which Force HQ had had their cave. Shortly, the lookout reported that he could see two parties of our troops carrying white flags going towards Sphakia.

I sent a man to the nearest party asking them what was happening – the answer came back that we had capitulated to the Germans at 5.30 am on 1st June and all resistance had ceased.[12] We were to march to Sphakia under a white flag. So this was the end.

I had thought it possible that we might escape to Egypt; I had thought it highly likely in Stylos that we would be killed; and at other times one hardly expected to get away without being at least wounded – but NEVER did the thought cross my mind that I should be taken prisoner.

Needless to say, Force HQ had all got away and must have known all about it on the evening of 31st May when I was there – they might have told me. Lt Col. Rooke also got away and I wonder if he ever thought of us at all – or ever thinks of us now: I am still waiting for his order to move from Stylos!

I ordered all rifles to be destroyed and all steel helmets thrown away (we were told anyone in possession of a steel helmet would be shot by the Germans). Myself, I threw my pistol into the sea and smashed my own beautiful pair of Zeiss[13] by swinging them round my head and then hard down on the rocks! It was now that I realised I had lost my gold ring[14] – about all I have left to lose! I know how I lost it now: when we spent the night in Askifou Plain I remember emptying my haversack of all unnecessary articles and then, thinking we were bound for Egypt, I threw away soap, etc., and also a bottle of Dettol.[15] However, I washed my hands in this first and they were probably a little greasy afterwards and so my signet ring must have pulled off. My finger was not as fat as it had been either!

Next we produced the whitest article we had between us, an old towel. I tied it to a stick and marched the two miles into Sphakia at the head of our sorry, downhearted, hungry party. There we met our first Germans, Bavarian Alpine Troops, who separated officers and men and rounded us up into groups. And so, at 12.00 noon on 1st June 1941, ended my liberty.

From : Lt-Col.O.P.JOCE, A.D.O.S.
        O.S.5.

                                    General Headquarters,
                                    Middle East, Cairo.

                                    7th June, 1941.

Dear *Mr. Casdagli*

        Brigadier Richards who is away on duty for a
day or two has told me to write and tell you how sorry
he is that we have still no news of the evacuation of your
son Major A.T. CASDAGLI from CRETE.

        The D.O.S. is very concerned about it, and we
are making every endeavour to ascertain further news of
him.   He was seen by other officers shortly before they
were evacuated.

        I will inform you as soon as I get further
news.

                            Yours *Sincerely*

                                    O.P. Joce

T.E. Casdagli Esq.,
P.O.Box, 275,
Cairo.

Letter to T. E. Casdagli, 7 June 1941.

2. FIRST DAYS OF CAPTIVITY

1st June 1941
Captured at Sphakia, on the south coast of Crete at noon. Started marching back to Chania at 4.00 pm arriving at Askifou for the night. Very tired.

2nd June 1941
Continued the march. So far our only food has been a quarter of a packet of biscuits and a quarter of a tin of bully at Vrises at 2.00 pm, after marching since 8.00 am. Spending the night in the ruins of Stylos. Saw again that ghastly olive grove.

3rd June 1941
Arrived at Chania at 3.00 pm. Marched on another few miles to Galatas, which has been turned into a transit camp area, using the site of the old Seventh General Hospital. Conditions are very unpleasant, the only saving grace being the close proximity of the sea. Food very scanty and irregular. Weather very hot, water also a problem. We are about three hundred officers here.

9th June 1941
Detailed to move and at 7.00 am were transported by lorry the nine miles to Maleme aerodrome. I shall never forget the sight. The whole area was a graveyard of German planes – mostly Ju-52s[1] piled high up into enormous mountains of wreckage. There were two hundred planes at least; we also saw some destroyed British planes. Even so, the Germans were not short of transport, although the planes were fairly ancient.

We were put ten officers to a plane and flown to Athens. The Ju-52 I was in was made in 1934, according to the plate fixed inside. We were roped into our seats and covered by a guard with a tommy gun. And so ended my seven months in Crete. A sad story but, in spite of all, some happy memories.

We flew very low over the sea. Arrived at Tatoi aerodrome, twelve and a half miles north of Athens, at 8.30 am. Transported by lorry from Tatoi to Athens. What a sad journey that was, passing through the well-known streets and seeing all the old haunts – but as a prisoner! Left Athens at 4.00 pm by train.

10th June 1941
Detrained at 2.00 am due to a break in the railway line. Marched all through the night and day until 1.30 pm. We just marched on automatically, halting

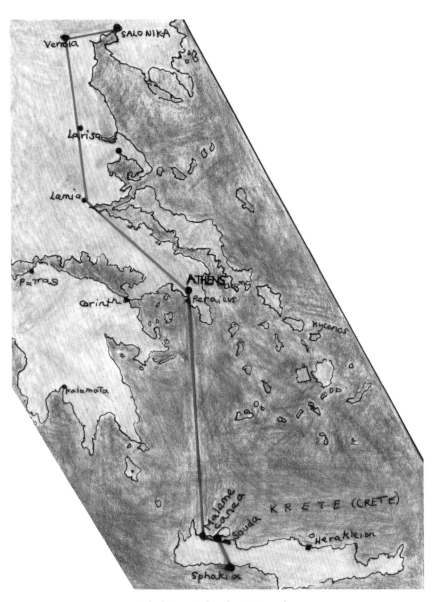

Sphakia to Salonika, 565 miles.

about ten minutes every two hours. The Germans promised to shoot ten officers for every one who tried to escape but we were all far too tired, weak and hungry to do much more than put one foot before the other. The march back from Sphakia was but a taste of what was to come and this forced march over the Bralos Pass really tested me.[2]

We had no food, only what we found along the way. The weakest fell out and were collected by the Germans and brought along in lorries. I did alright. I was shod in shoes, but they stood up really well. I managed to carry my pack with my very few remaining worldly possessions in it and my water bottle. The march was twenty-two miles and in fact for the last three I carried half of Leslie Akin's (RA) kit too. He was in a very bad way but we made it alright.

None of us will ever forget the kindness and sympathy of the Greek people we passed in the villages. Our miserable, bedraggled column was the object of their great generosity although they must feel we have 'let them down' though never by word or deed was it even hinted at. From them we got our only water and whatever food they had to spare they gave us. Had it not been for them, I do not like to think what state we should be in. One day I shall go over this road again and try and repay some of that kindness. It makes me prouder than ever to be Greek.

After crossing the Bralos Pass we dropped down to Lamia and before reaching the town turned left to a small railway junction. Our long trudge was over. We were entrained into cattle trucks, thirty-five to forty to a truck, to continue on to Larisa.

26 JUIN 1941

I am a prisoner of war and in good health. In the next letter I will give you my address. It is useless to write before receiving the new address.

With best wishes

Name and surname _____ ALEXIS T. CASDAGLI

Military rank: _____ MAJOR

Designation of military formation _____ R.A.O.C

Postcard home, 26 June 1941.

POST OFFICE
TELEGRAM

Charges to pay
s. ____ d.
RECEIVED

No.
OFFICE STAMP
PADDINGTON
8 JLY. 41
W.2

97 2

Prefix. Time handed in. Office of Origin and Service Instructions. Words.

From _____ 95 _____ 395 12.15 LIVERPOOL Y OHMS 36 To _____

IRS A T CASDAGLI C/O MRS MARTINEAU FLAT 8 97 LINDEN
GARDENS LONDON W 2 =

REGRET TO INFORM YOU CAPT A T CASDAGLI RAOC IS REPORTED
PRISONER OF WAR LETTER FOLLOWS = UNDER SECRETARY OF
STATE FOR WAR + 8

For free repetition of doubtful words telephone "TELEGRAMS ENQUIRY" or call, with this form
at office of delivery. Other enquiries should be accompanied by this form and, if possible, the envelope.

B or C
C

Telegram to Joyce, 8 July 1941.

3. A REAL NIGHTMARE

11th June 1941

We stayed the night in our trucks at Larisa as the railway line was broken again. In the morning we marched a mile or two before entraining for Salonika, again in cattle trucks. Our journey was only eventful for the shooting of three officers, Rossiter (Cyprus Regiment), Reeves (RAF), and Herman (Commandos). The shots came whistling past our carriage. At every station the local people tried their hardest to throw us food and it was for accepting it that the guards fired down the train. Herman was hit in the wrist and Rossiter and Reeves in the head.

We arrived hot, hungry and tired at 5.00 pm. Our impression of Salonika[1] was naturally not of the best, added to the fact that it was pouring in torrents. We were soon soaked to the skin as most of us were in shorts and shirts. We marched out to the Pavlos Melas Barracks[2] where we found a huge prisoners' transit camp.

The conditions are past all belief. Nearly all the rooms are bug-ridden and practically every officer (though fortunately not myself) is lousy. For the first time since capture we are to be on regular rations which are: one ninth of a loaf of bread, three quarters of an army biscuit (Greek type), one ladle of soup and two cups of herb tea per man per day. Incidentally, on the train from Larisa we had been given Greek army biscuits and salted fish – not adequate to appease our hunger but it tasted simply wonderful.

14th June 1941

We are expecting daily to be moved to Germany from here, as we are the only officers and all the previous batches have been sent on by train to Germany.

17th June 1941

The ration store was raided today by some British troops, prisoners of course, and as a result our rations have been cut to half for the next three days.

19th June 1941

We are now four hundred and fifty officers, all from Crete, and several thousand men. We are kept separate of course. We sleep on bedsteads but as there is no bedding it is almost more comfortable to sleep on the floor. It is possible to buy certain articles of clothing from some of the troops and I have bought a shirt, a blanket and a great coat (five hundred drachmas) – it

WHAT
THE RED CROSS
IS — AND WHAT IT DOES

FOR the duration of the War the British Red Cross Society and the Order of St. John are working together as a War Organisation to care for wounded and sick soldiers, sailors, merchant seamen and airmen, civilian air-raid victims, prisoners of war and civilian internees.

★ To-day over three hundred thousand personnel trained by the Red Cross and St. John are serving at home and abroad. In addition, many thousands of men and women have been trained by them.

★ Over 100 emergency medical stores have been established throughout this country.

★ Many hundreds of ambulances, mobile X-ray and physio-therapy vans, etc., have been provided.

★ Hospitals and convalescent homes have been organised, equipped and staffed.

★ First-aid posts for the shipwrecked are maintained all around our coasts.

★ Sick and wounded men of the fighting services and air-raid victims are tended and provided with extra comforts.

★ Prisoners of war and civilians interned in enemy countries are sent regular parcels of food, clothing, tobacco, books and medical supplies.

★ The missing are traced in co-operation with the International Red Cross Committee at Geneva.

★ Help is given to relations desiring to visit dangerously sick and wounded soldiers, sailors, and airmen, and of civilians injured by enemy action.

★ Thousands of Red Cross Postal Messages are sent and received weekly between the British Empire and enemy occupied territories. These are often the only link between members of widely scattered families.

These activities of the Red Cross and St. John War Organisation, and others too, are financed from the Duke of Gloucester's Fund. But more money is needed, much more, if " The Red Cross " is to carry on its work and meet its steadily increasing responsibilities.

THE RED CROSS & ST. JOHN
need every penny you can spare
Send your Donation to
H.R.H. the Duke of Gloucester's Fund
St. James's Palace, London, S.W.1

This appeal is made on behalf of the War Organisation of the British Red Cross Society and the Order of St. John of Jerusalem. Registered under the War Charities Act,1940.
P.T.O.

Red Cross pamphlet.

is much more to carry but the money is no use to me and I feel that this is a good investment as, although it is roasting hot now, the winter in Germany may be severe.

10th July 1941

We have had one false alarm to move and have been transferred to another part of these barracks where conditions are even worse and where water is even scarcer and there are no bedsteads. Just bug-ridden huts.[3] Most people are suffering from dysentery – almost everyone is lousy and everyone without exception is famished. The Greek Red Cross[4] have been allowed on two occasions to bring us a tiny quantity of food, which made an enormous difference to us – particularly in knowing that some kind people are still thinking of us. We are all feeling pretty low and very weak.

18th July 1941

Seven Palestinian troops were shot last night trying to escape. The Germans got to know of their plan, lay up for them and tommy-gunned them in the camp. One was shot crossing the parade ground and had been left there when we paraded in the morning, no doubt 'pour encourager les autres'.[5] The Germans now pay us fifty-four marks per month.[6]

As a rule I get up at 5.10 am ready for 6.00 am parade. At 7.00 am a cup of herb tea (virtually undrinkable). At 10.30 am someone gives a lecture to pass the time, even I have lectured on 'Cotton'.[7] Lunch, the big event of the day, is at noon when we get a ladle of soup. Horse meat is quite wholesome and delicious when you are as hungry as we are. Issue of rations at 2.00 pm. Tea, 5.30 pm – another cup of herb tea. Evening parade at 6.00 pm. Turn in at 9.00 pm. An interminably long day when books are very few and far between and one is ever and continually hungry. Conditions so bad one almost looks forward to going to Germany rather than be here longer than necessary. These last five weeks have been a real nightmare.

The cloth-counting glass.

Sliding door

35 men

Typed diagram of the 'accommodation' in Casdagli's cattle truck.

4. CATTLE TRUCK JOURNEY

22nd July 1941

Definite order to move given today. We were all searched. Our last remaining possessions whittled down even further. I had taken from me a penknife, cap-badge, and a small cloth-counting glass[1] that belonged to Grandfather. We were given four days' rations consisting of Yugoslav meat in tins and Greek army biscuits.

At 5.00 pm we marched out of the Pavlos Melas Barracks, about three hundred and fifty British officers. At Salonika station two hundred Cypriot prisoners of war joined us to entrain for Germany.[2] The 'accommodation' is cattle trucks with no straw nor facilities for obtaining drinking water nor any sanitary arrangements whatsoever. Approximately thirty per cent of our strength are suffering from dysentery in either slight or serious form, while seventy per cent (judging from my truck and other information obtained) are suffering from diarrhoea. The numbers in each truck vary but the average is thirty-two. In our truck there are thirty-five.

29th July 1941

The journey was made with the sliding doors permanently shut and locked. The only ventilation was from two small slit windows just above head height over which barbed wire had been nailed. On an average we were let out for ten minutes every twenty-four hours but on one occasion we were not allowed out for thirty-six hours.

At Belgrade the train stopped in a siding for two hours and the doors were opened. The ladies of the Yugoslav Red Cross were excessively kind and gave us each two biscuits, a razor blade, a few cigarettes. They also fetched us drinking water. Three of our number were detained in hospital being too weak to go any further, incidentally, thus making conditions less awful for the remainder.

Our rations for the trip had been a Greek army biscuit and one third of a tin of M & V[3] (Yugoslav) per day. We also had one seventh of a Greek loaf per day. With the great heat in the trucks and the complete lack of movement or any form of exercise, I personally never felt hungry. We had to use our mess tins for relieving nature and these had to be emptied through the slit windows. Luckily, I was in good health but it is not difficult to imagine the sufferings of those with dysentery and diarrhoea. The stench was terrible.

These conditions lasted practically a FULL WEEK. Leaving Salonika on 22nd July, we arrived at Lübeck today, our route being Veles, Skopje, Belgrade,

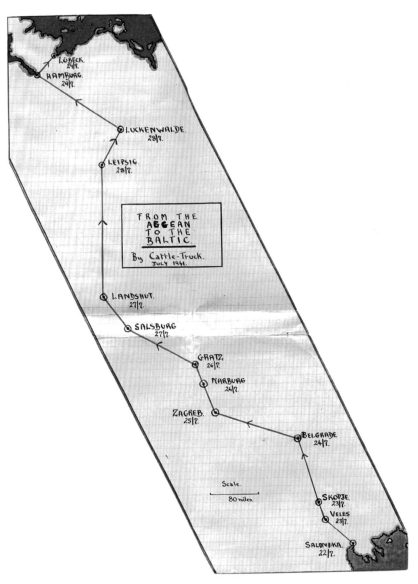

Cattle truck journey from the Aegean to the Baltic Sea.

Zagreb, Marburg, Grätz, Landshut, Leipzig, Luckenwalde, Hamburg, Lübeck.[4] We had our first taste of RAF raids in a siding at Hamburg. We had nothing to read, no playing cards, etc. It is difficult to realise that the time actually did pass – the incredible discomfort kept us awake most of the time. Still, we tried to make the best of it. At our end of the truck we managed to cut a very small hole in the floor and through this we swept all the dust and dirt, had organised 'meal' times, etc.

We were pretty fagged out and stiff when we got to Lübeck[5] at 8.00 am but reasonably cheerful. Again it was our luck to arrive in the rain! Detrained and we were drawn up in columns of fives. From the station we had a three-mile march to our first German prison camp: Oflag X-C.[6]

OFLAG X-C, LÜBECK

Identity tag.

View, Oflag X-C. © ICRC

Huts, Oflag X-C. © ICRC

Altar, Oflag X-C. © ICRC

5. PRISONER 3311

29th July 1941

Oflag X-C Lübeck is a new camp[1] and we are the only occupants, although it will hold many more than our four hundred and twenty. We must have left at least thirty officers in various hospitals on the train journey. We were given lunch in the open, some potatoes and a stew, which seemed marvellous to us.

We were then paraded and inspected by the German officers to see which of us were Jews! Later we were deloused, searched and given our POW number on an aluminium disc which must be worn at all times. Mine is X-C 3311. I was also given a metal identity tag.[2] I should mention here that there is a Greek General among us, General Kaffatos, who was caught in Crete and is apparently being treated as a British officer, although he belongs to the Greek army. He did the cattle truck journey with us being granted no privileges due to his rank at all – from all accounts, he is a very stout-hearted fellow.[3]

30th July 1941

We were allotted our permanent rooms today and I am in Room 4, Block 11, together with Tishy Murray (Black Watch), Ken Hardie (Rangers), Lambert (RASC), Wolstenholme (RA) and dear Jack Hamson (Gen. List),[4] all majors except Jack who is a captain.[5]

3rd August 1941

Heavy bombing raid by the RAF last night.[6] A good deal of heavy AA in the vicinity. Our rations are very meagre but we can sometimes get a little tinned food through the canteen, but it does not go far among the lot of us. We get one fifth of a German loaf a day and no biscuits.

4th August 1941

No facilities have yet been granted to us for writing home. I have however sent a postcard from Salonika. I expect they are worrying.

7th August 1941

Old Jones, over sixty, one of the few Merchant Seamen in our party, was today shot by the machine gun from one of the towers – four bullets in his back. He actually had one foot over the wire in an attempt to retrieve a football; he actually fell inside the parade ground, which shows how far he trespassed! He was taken off to the hospital in the town and we hope he will live.[7]

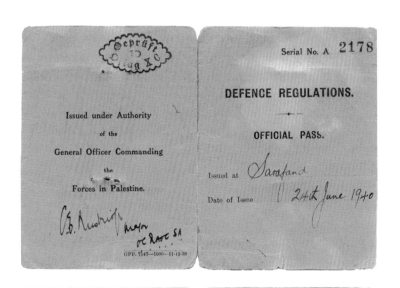

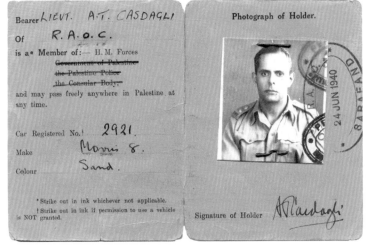

Army pass with Oflag X-C stamp.

<u>8th August 1941</u>
Another RAF raid last night – a good deal of AA. We are getting a little tinned fish and tomatoes from the canteen, which is a very welcome addition to our watery lunchtime soup.

<u>9th August 1941</u>
Today wrote two postcards, one to Joyce in London and the other to Mum in Cairo. They tell us Red Cross parcels are expected soon. Very exciting.

<u>13th August 1941</u>
We were inspected today by a German General. Parade in the morning was at 8.00 am instead of 9.00 am. Evening parade is at 8.00 pm.

<u>16th August 1941</u>
Eighteen more officers are in from Crete via Salonika where apparently things went from bad to worse. Three more people were shot trying to escape,[8] and two RAMC orderlies[9] were shot for hanging out their washing on the barbed wire – all killed.

We made a complaint today about our rations, which are very small and poor in quality.[10] The weather is a little warmer but generally cold and damp.

<u>18th August 1941</u>
The two blankets which we have been issued were today withdrawn and we were given one small half-cotton blanket four feet by six feet. Incidentally, my blanket which I had lugged all the way from Salonika was confiscated here, as were everyone else's private blankets – no receipts given. With this cold weather it will mean sleeping in a greatcoat and hoping for the best. Those without any thick clothes are wishing they had bought them at Salonika – my only bad investment was the blanket.

<u>20th August 1941</u>
Complaints have produced the re-issue of one more blanket. We were also given some more postcards for home. Our block has now been divided into two and we are only twenty-two officers in our half. More officers are expected at the camp. We were given some French biscuits in our rations today. Quite good but small.

<u>21st August 1941</u>
Had our weekly hot shower today; wrote some more cards home but no letters in the camp yet from UK.

| 1 | 2 | 3 | 4 | 5 | 6 | 7 | 8 | 9 | 10 | 11 | 12 | 13 | 14 | 15 | 16 | 17 | 18 | 19 | 20 | 21 | 22 | 23 | 24 | 25 |

Personalkarte I: Personelle Angaben

Beschriftung der Erkennungsmarke

Kriegsgefangenen=Stammlager: **Oflag X C** I 11/4.

Lager: **Oflag X C** Nr. 3311

Name: **Casdagli**	Staatsangehörigkeit: **Engländer**
Vorname: **Alexis Theodore**	Dienstgrad: **Major d.R.**
Geburtstag und -ort: **10.4.06, Manchester**	Truppenteil: **Kraftfahrtruppe** Komp. usw.: **M.E.F.**
Religion: **Church of England**	Zivilberuf: **Kaufmann** Berufs-Gr.:
Vorname des Vaters: **Theodore**	Matrikel Nr. (Stammrolle des Heimatstaates): **Kairo**
Familienname der Mutter: **Ralli**	Gefangennahme (Ort und Datum): **Kreta, 1.6.41**
	Ob gesund, krank, verwundet eingeliefert: **gesund**

Lichtbild

Nähere Personalbeschreibung

Größe	Haarfarbe	Besondere Kennzeichen:
5'10"	schwarz	keine

Fingerabdruck des rechten(!) Zeigefingers

Name und Anschrift der zu benachrichtigenden Person in der Heimat des Kriegsgefangenen

Mrs. A.T. Casdagli, c/o Messrs. E. Casdagli & Sons, 32 Oxford Street, Manchester,1, England.

Wenden!

Beschriftung der Erkennungsmarke Nr. 3311

Lager: **Oflag X C**

Charaktereigenschaften u. a.	Besondere Fähigkeiten	Sprachkenntnisse	Führung

Datum	Grund der Bestrafung	Strafmaß	Verbüßt, Datum

Schutzimpfungen während der Gefangenschaft gegen — Erkrankungen

Pocken	Sonstige Impfungen (Typhus, Ruhr, Cholera usw.)	Krankheit	Revier von	bis	Lazarett — Krankenhaus von	bis
27. Aug. 1941 am 27.8.41						
Erfolg	gegen					
am	am					
Erfolg	gegen					
am am 19.9.41 am						
Erfolg	gegen gegen					
	am am					
	gegen gegen					

Datum	Grund der Versetzung	Neues Kr.-Gef.-Lager	Datum	Grund der Versetzung	Neues Kr.-Gef.-Lager
8. Okt. 1941	VKH Qu. Vef. 6376/41	Oflag VI C			
15 Jan. 1942	OKW Vef. 18.12.41	Oflag IX A			
2.3.44	O.K.W. 15.2.44	Oflag IX B			

POW record showing inoculations and vaccinations.

46

<u>27th August 1941</u>
I was issued today with a French army tunic. Lately we have been getting batches of RAF officers in and more arrived today; they total about one hundred and twenty. Most of them have been recently shot down and bring us the latest news of the outside world. Inoculated TAB and also vaccinated today.

<u>29th August 1941</u>
Made a nightlight out of some brown boot polish sold at the canteen – useless as polish but a great success as fuel for my lamp.

<u>4th September 1941</u>
Our room was deloused today as several had again got lice. This operation lasted from 12.50 pm until 8.00 pm. In the process I had my cap taken by the Germans, very upsetting as Joyce had sent it to me in 1939 in Cairo from London and, although much worn, was a beauty. Fancy still having lice after being here five weeks. We hope this second disinfecting will do the trick.

<u>5th September 1941</u>
The German Commandant's seventy-fifth birthday was celebrated today by a military band playing in the German part of the camp.[11] Today I noticed a swelling in my groin and I went to the Medical Officer about it. It is a rupture or hernia – apparently brought about by undue strain while in a weak condition – and the two alternatives are an operation or wearing a truss.[12] The Medical Officer is Lt Knight RN. He tells me I must be careful about lifting weights, etc., and is going to try and get me operated on in the town.

<u>8th September 1941</u>
Large-scale air raid in the district last night. Many incendiary bombs fell in the camp setting several huts on fire.[13] The German officers' mess, the German canteen, also our parcel store (no parcels in it luckily) were completely burnt out. Thirteen incendiaries fell through the roof of the camp hospital. Tony Holden had his leg broken and suffering from bad wound – taken to the town hospital – many narrow escapes. The fires were not put out till quite late in the day. The raid took place at 1.00 am. We were inoculated today for the second time. Our canteen has been closed.

<u>12th September 1941</u>
My cap was restored to me today, which has pleased me very much. I have now a pair of German jackboots, on loan; I shall try and buy them if I can as my shoes are practically done for.

Kriegsgefangenenpost
For Prisoner of War

Postkarte
Postcard

An

das Internationale Komitee vom Roten Kreuz

1 5 SEPT. 1941

Genf

Palais du Conseil général

Schweiz

Gebührenfrei!
Free postage

Kriegsgefangenenlager **Oflag X C** *Gef. No3309* Datum *2 - 9 - 1941*
Prisoner of War Camp   Date

Name *KAFFATOS*   Vorname *SOLON*
Surname   Christian Name

Dienstgrad u. Truppenteil *GREEK GENERAL*
Rank and Unit

Geburtsdatum *November 1888* Geburtsort *RETTIMO Crete*
Date of birth   Native-place

Letzter Wohnort *Village "Skiné, Canea Region (CRETE)*
Last dwelling

Adresse meiner Angehörigen *Katina Kaffatos-Skiné-Canea.Crete*
Home Address

(GREECE)

Unverwundet — leicht verwundet — in deutsche Kriegsgefangenschaft geraten —
Unwounded — slightly wounded — prisoner of war in Germany —

befinde mich wohl.
I am well

(Nichtzutreffendes ist zu streichen)   *J. Kaffatos*
(Passages non apposite to the point to be cancelled)   Signature

General Kaffatos' capture card, 11 September 1941.

14th September 1941
Third and last inoculation today.

16th September 1941
Since the bombing of the camp, the orderlies have been put on to clearing up the mess and have been forbidden to wait on the officers. We have been told we must clean our own rooms, passages, latrines, etc.[14] We have refused, so all public rooms and classrooms have been closed until either we decide to clean them or the orderlies have finished their cleaning up for the Germans.

20th September 1941
At long last the Germans are allowing us to take over our cookhouse. The Germans refuse to recognise Colonel Young[15] as our Senior British Officer but we will not recognise anyone else as he is the Senior British Officer. Still no lectures or classes. Our only relaxation is a few books, which are very much sought after. We are now being issued with a small piece of margarine instead of the previous fat. The Germans have not given us a ration scale so we do not know to what we are entitled. For instance, we get no sugar.[16] Still no signs of Red Cross parcels. Air raids now fail to wake us up at nights. I am keeping a record of how many have been heard by us.

21st September 1941
Have been able to buy the German boots and, although they are very much worn, they will be invaluable in the wet and snow.

24th September 1941
Was late for parade in the evening as I was in the RAF block and did not hear the whistle. I was reprimanded by the German officer! Rumours that this camp, at present four hundred and fifty Army and two hundred RAF, will be built up to over two thousand to make way in other camps for Russian prisoners.[17] The naval personnel were moved some time ago, but the RAF keep increasing in batches of thirty.

30th September 1941
Still no parcels, or any more officers. Some letters from home, however, have come in through Geneva. Still no agreement with the Germans over the cleaning of room and latrines. I have made two excellent little cooking stoves out of some old tins. The model was produced by a New Zealander and is a great success, burns paper or wood chippings. It will boil a mess tin in four minutes. I also made one for General Kaffatos, the Greek General who has

his room next to ours and whom I help quite a lot one way and another, owing to the language difficulty. He knows not a word of English and only a little French. He has written material for two lectures on Crete which I have translated into English and they will be delivered when the lectures restart. The library has now been increased which is a great joy. We still continue to be very, very hungry.

2nd October 1941
Lectures restarted today and we have won our point. Delivered the first of General Kaffatos's lectures to a full house – very well received. Like everyone else, I seem to think and dream of food all day.

3rd October 1941
Today I had my first letter from Menda.[18] There was no postmark and I rather think it must have been sent through some German billeted[19] on her.

7th October 1941
No parcels yet issued; some more mail has arrived. Rumour that the whole of this camp leaves tomorrow.[20]

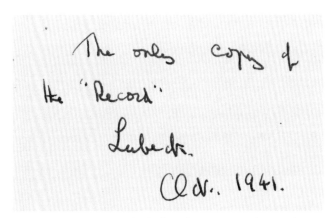

Several POWs worked all night on 7 October 1941
producing *The Record*, published here for the first time.

THE LÜBECK RECORD

| Oflag X-C | 7 October 1941 | 10 pfennig |

At the final moment when we learn that our first issue is to be our last, The Record is having to rush into print, mostly rewritten, very much improvised, but still we hope useful as a souvenir issue. Its general air was to have been the relation for ourselves to the future of our present strange common interests, to record them for the day when we shall be able to push our chairs a little further from the table, light a cigarette that did not cost a week's jam ration and laugh as we reminisce on the things we did, thought about, talked of, hoped for and even cooked. From contributions, we hoped to get into these few sheets a touch of our homelands, the places and things of good memories. **The Record** was to have served as a diary of prison camp life for all its subscribers.

This issue, typed on a German typewriter in a great hurry, is but the shadow of what the substance was planned to be. We can only hope that **The Record** will be truly born again elsewhere. Meanwhile, with frantic energy, our tame laureate has squeezed the following from his Muse...

IN MEMORIAM

I think that Lübeck's spires I'll see
When I get back to Innisfree
Or Bermondsey
Or way across the Tasman sea
They'll bring back memories to me
Of rumours in the lavat'ry
Of rumours at the cookhouse door
Waiting in the queue and dreaming
Waiting for our hot and steaming
Rumours we have heard before
Queen Ann is dead
How did she die?
Raising her right hand
Just like I!
They say there's fifty pounds of mail
Red Cross parcels without fail
The Russian Army's on its way
Berlin was flattened yesterday
And all the other things they say
Now Lübeck's spires green and gay
Neath the horizon fade away
Oflag X-C's beyond the blue
The last confounded rumour's true
We're off!

CAMP DIARY

19 September was one of the most notable days in the camp's recent calendar. Then Capt. G. Hook, New Zealand Expeditionary Force, and Capt. H. Heaton, Pioneer Corps, took over the jobs of Camp Messing Officer and Camp Quartermaster respectively. With nine English orderlies, they took over the cookhouse, their day's work to cook and issue the day's rations to 703 English officers and men. A few other record-worthy dates, taken at random, were: 7 Sept. Fire in the camp, one English officer wounded. 10—12 Sept. More RAF arrived. 17 Sept. Bedboard parade. 18 Sept. Sixteen new Army officers arrived, including a dentist. 19 Sept. Margarine ration replaced fat rations. English took over the cookhouse. 21 Sept. Noodle soup. Sunbathing weather all this week. 23 Sept. Pea soup. Jam and Limburger cheese as weekly ration. Oct. 1 ?c (blast this typewriter) First general coal issue. Eight blocks of coal per day for a large room, six for others. Rice soup. 2 Oct. Cabbage soup. 3 Oct. Salt fish (stock fish) sauce and double potato ration. 4 Oct. Pea soup. 5 Oct. Macaroni soup. 6 Oct. Sauce of soya bean extract and potatoes. 7 Oct. Cabbage soup. Oct. 8........?.....

LETTERS

Here are some of the first few slender extracts from letters. The first four are from home, the remainder from neutral subscribers to the International Red Cross. All have passed German censorship.

'--baby's second tooth has at last broken through. He looks just like you now--'

'--the Deanna Durbin marriage is said to be just another Hollywood flop after all--'

'--the Germans were always pretty good at sausage-making so I suppose you get plenty of it--'

'--this has been a frightful August for weather in England--'

These letters are printed exactly as written: 21.8.41. From Holland. 'My name is Maud (I am a girl) and I am eighteen years old. I am tolerable tall and slender, have blue eyes and fair hairs (without a permanent) and little pits in my cheeks when I laugh. (What a beauty I seem to be is it not?) I hope you like the parcel. Its not so much because I get no money any more from my parents, thats impossible so you understand that I cannot pay so much more. The tea I send you had I my mother send me in one of her letters from America so you understand that it is very dear!--' 14.8.41. Holland. 'This morning I went to the Red Cross and asked for a prisoner of war which I should like to send something eatable, and a letter to make him the things easier to undergo. I am a student on the economic university of Rotterdam. My mother has died in August last year. But when I think of what she has to undergo now, I think it is for her the best way. I hope this letter will reach you also my parcel containing a tin containing something to eat which I hope you should like. If you have some special wishes please write it to me. If I can get it I will send it.' 11.8.41. 'We are two sisters and since two years we live in Holland. Before were in Dutch India where it is very fine. Now we cannot go back. Tell us what you like very much and we shall try and get it. It is not today very easy to become many things (But we shall do our best) We admire your aviators very much.'

13.8.41. From a girl law student at Leiden: 'It is difficult now to make up a parcel because there are lots of things either unobtainable or for which coupons must be given. However I have laid up a little store of cigarettes, chocolate, soap and other things, I have given up my months jam coupon and so I am able to send you some real English marmalade!'

THIS letter is from an officer's sister in Athens and is particularly interesting: 'The Red Cross won't accept any more parcels. My mother-in-law's small house has been commandeered by the Germans and my sister-in-law's by the Italians. I am very much thinner. Baby is really fine and growing rapidly. Owing to the kindness of the Germans no-one is hungry here—'

SPORTS

This is the situation in the Camp Basketball Competition on 7 October, the teams are known by their Captains' names: P/O Simmonds 11 points; F-Lt Jacquier 9 pts; Maj. Marshall 8 pts; Lt Leigh 7 pts; Orderlies 6 pts; Lt Quartermain 4 pts; P/O Prowse 4 pts; Lt McRobbie

---

3 pts; F/O Valachos 2 pts; Maj. Ford 3 games played, no points.

LECTURES

This programme is now just one of the plans of mice and men. But well worth recording. September 6: Rugby Club, Inter Services, International; Sarawak under the White Rajah by Lt Howie; A Day in the Port of London by Maj. Godden; Crete (Part 2) by General Kaffatos; Art for Ourselves by F/O Dilly; The Libyan Campaign by Lt Col. Campbell DSO.

OLD COMRADES

The Captains and the Kings departed
In boats across the Cretan sea,
Leaving behind them, heavy-hearted,
Such simple folk as you and me.

We hear they've been promoted, fêted,
We hear that X received a Mention
And dear old Y's been decorated
And Z has got a colonel's pension.
And brightly glows in blue and rose
The splendour of their DSOs.

We hear of them urbane and hearty
Unbending with a glass of fizz
Or condescending at a party
In aid of Prisoners Charities.
(If they had known a German 'jug'
Would they, we ask, be quite so smug?)

Nothing can shake them, firmly rooted.
Their proud self-confidence will stand.
Well fed, well polished, spurred and booted
They'll greet us kindly when we land.
Yet here and there a cheek may burn
When certain wanderers, like us, return.

EXCHANGE AND MART

Oflag X-C's market has been one of the world's most unstable. After a lot of painstaking research, combined with a little profitable speculation on the side, our Financial Reporter has produced the list of exchange rates below using cigarettes as a common currency.

They show average maximum and minimum prices. They are pre–Red Cross parcel prices and we shall never look upon their like again. New influxes of RAF loaded with treasure (so there have been reports) have occasionally knocked the market sideways. But it will be no good storming our office saying these prices are wrong. They are records of actual deals. Freak deals have been included: 1 mess tin for a promised pair of artificial silk vest and pants; 10 marks (about 1 3/4d) for one cheese ration; 1 mark (about 1/4d) for a cigarette. Bread has been the highest basis for exchange, camp money the lowest and cigarettes the most usual. Types on the market have recently included English, French, Belgian, Yugoslav, Polish American, Greek, Turkish, Portuguese, American, Dutch, Canadian.

	Maximum Price Given In Cigarettes	Minimum Price Given In Cigarettes
Bread ration	40	10
Biscuit ration	3 for 2	1
Potatoes	2 for a Large one	1 for a small
Large billy can	60	40
Round billy can	35	20
Hag Cola	2	
Hamburger sauce	10	
Margarine ration	6	
Thermos flask	30	
Pullover	50	
Sausage	4	
Fat ration	4	
Pea soup	15	
Jam ration	10	5
Cheese ration	10	5
Bottle of beer	5	2
Rubber pillow	50	
Rhubarb wine	10	5
Five fig biscuits	15	5

OFLAG COOKERY BOOK

Lt Howard Goodwin offers the following
as the RECIPE OF THE WEEK.

JAM PUDDING LÜBECK

Take three parts of breadcrumbs, a quarter of them toasted, to one part of mashed potato. Mix in one packet of Hag-Cola, the caffeine-free coffee substitute bought in the canteen, or half a week's jam ration.

Moisten to a dough. Steam the result in a tightly covered bowl for half an hour. The result will have the consistency and taste (!) of plum pudding. To make STEAK AND KIDNEY PUDDING LÜBECK, substitute one ration of liver sausage for the sweetening and cook in the same way. Says Lt Goodwin, 'Close your eyes when eating and it really IS steak and kidney pudding!'

RECOMMENDED FOR COFFEE. One half-round of bread, toasted until it is black and burning and rolled to a fine powder with a bottle and board. This makes two cups. The coffee must be boiled until the bread grains have sunk to the bottom. Canteen chestnuts burned until they give off a bitter acrid smoke and then ground are just as good. Sweet Wood licorice root (Sussholz), boiled and filtered makes a good, sweet, hot drink.

(The Editor is not responsible for statements made by correspondents, but will accept cooking samples.)

MY FAVOURITE PUB
No. 1

We used to call it 'The Cheese'. To American tourists it was 'The Cheshire Cheese'. Its main attraction to them was that they could go and help to make the brass-plated corner seat in the cosy sawdust-floored eating room where Samuel Johnson sat, a little more shiny while they ate enormous helpings of famous steak pie.

The Cheese was in a narrow alleyway off Fleet St, just near the corner tobacco shop where they still sell snuff by the ton to the printers.

Old Samuel Johnson puffing his way asthmatically up to the Cheese for a bottle of claret would go in there and sit on a snuff barrel –– they still have it –– surrounded by the yellow, brown and gold filled snuff jars. To us the small bar, full of old shiny crooked wood and a blazing fire, was a good hideout from the frantic night news editors sending copy boys around to pipe our names in every bar in the Street from Poppins to the Falstaff, via the Bull. They had an old ale at the Cheese. It cost one and twopence for a pint in a battered old pewter mug. Foolish strangers would order a pint and drink it down like light ale. Then they would begin to think they were good drinkers because there was no immediate effect. So they would have another. Half an hour later London town would begin to go round and round. Old ale has a delayed action kick.

In spite of the Americans, the Cheese had never lost, or consciously tried to keep, its atmosphere of Johnsonian warmth and mellow old English ways. The panelled walls of the bar were hung with glistening catches of fish. Above the fireplace was an oil painting of an old waiter who had served half a lifetime there. On the table beside it was a noisy alcoholic old parrot that seemed to live for free beer. In the passage outside, the waiters yelled food orders up the crooked stairs and drink orders down to the cellar. There was no modern new-fangled nonsense about lifts and speaking tubes there.

Outside, over the worn stone steps and down the alley, hummed the Street that never sleeps; where the newspaper vans make traffic jams at two o'clock every morning.

BUT the Cheese is no more. Last year a simple domestic fire destroyed it. And so the shade of Johnson, with the attendant shadow of Boswell cocking a listening ear, will hover no more around the steaming trolley loads of unforgettable steak pie.

<u>Stop The Press!</u>

The Muse, feeling particularly boisterous, has just slipped
in with this:

<u>Z-O-OPER & SPUDS</u>

Kartoffel and soup, z-o-oper and spuds
Big ones and small ones, frostbitten and duds,
We fry, bake and stew, boil and pretend
That they're not what we KNOW we shall taste in the end
Z-o-oper and spuds
Kartoffel and soup.

With fond hopes we awake at the dawn of each day
With our faith to the cookhouse we hurry away
Then back to our barracks we carefully troop
Bearing bowls of kartoffel, spuds, z-o-oper, soup.

When I dine at the Ritz at the end of the war
And the waiter respectfully offers me more
Of the beefsteak, I fear I may bashfully droop
Murmuring dreamily, 'Z-o-oper, spuds, soup.'

Kartoffel and soup, z-o-oper and spuds
Gritty ones, broken ones, tattered ones, duds.
They make pies, cutlets, rolls, meals big or small
That we know when we've had them were just after all
— Kartoffel and soup
Z-o-oper and spuds –

Kartoffel and soup, z-o-oper and spuds
When homeward bound, sweethearts joyfully meet us
They'll cry with dismay as they hurry to greet us
'Why — he's only kartoffel
Z-O-oper and spuds! —'

FOR THE TRAIN HOME
(How long O Lord —-)

Here is a crossword puzzle for the train home. Draw out a square and draw ten vertical and ten horizontal lines across it. You have 100 squares. Number them from left to right starting from the top. The following are black squares: Nos. 1, 10, 17, 34, 31, 39, 45, 47, 50, 51, 54, 56, 62, 70, 77, 84, 91 and 100. Here are the clues for the rest:

ACROSS 2. Merry quip and jest. 11. Urge. 18. A kind of Baptist. 21. One gets it on knuckles. 35. Goes with honours. 32. Elapsed interval (two words). 41. He and his kind were friends with Persians. 48. Conjunction. 52. Half an Easter food. 57. Bad things in parts. 63. A jumble of letters, an offence against the King rearranged. 71. Ancient city. 78. A singular girl's name. 81. Distant. 85. The blue one is worth having. 92. A middle class vocalist.

DOWN 2. Don't shoot him. 3. A boarding house veg. 4. Half a game of chance. 5. Dies ——. 6. The sort of meal we want. 9. Finish. 11. A messenger of sorts. 20. You will feel one if you can't guess. 27. Common on motorcars and hotels. 34. Me. 49. Common abbreviation of a female saint. 55. Eastern lovely. 57. Indefinite. 61. Per ardua. 64. 52 across. 66. What an exhaust does to smoke. 72. They used to be called. 80. This year. 87. Christian name of a shepherdess.

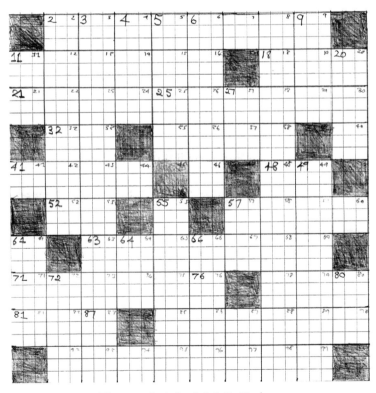

The puzzle is by Maj. L. Parker

OFLAG VI-B, DÖSSEL-WARBURG

Oflag VI-B, Dössel-Warburg, on a high desolate plateau, originally intended as a military airfield, opened in September 1940 for French officers. They were joined by virtually all the British POWs officers in Germany. © ICRC

Visit of Dr Schirmer, ICRC, 15 October 1941. © ICRC

Dr Schirmer with Generals Fortune and Somerset. © ICRC

6. FUCK HITLER![1]

<u>8th October 1941</u>
Whole of Oflag X-C moved today. Lunch was at 10.00 am and two days' dry rations being taken (two thirds of a loaf and some blood sausage). We were ready to move at 12.30 pm. Marched about a mile carrying all our kit and entrained into cattle trucks in a siding, forty officers plus two guards in each truck. There were benches however in the trucks. Left at 3.50 pm

<u>9th October 1941</u>
Arrived at Dössel-Warburg, Westphalia, after a very trying night sitting up the whole time. Again carrying all our kit, we had about a three-mile march to a huge hutted camp at Dössel, Oflag VI-B. Coffee given us in the evening. By the way, our route from Lübeck was Lübeck, Buchen, Altenbeken, Warburg, Dössel.[2] There are sixteen of us majors in one room – very crowded.[3] No water laid on and only earth latrines. Have up to date received seven letters. Six RAF officers escaped on the way from Lübeck by cutting a hole in the carriage in the night and jumping out.[4]

<u>11th October 1941</u>
Gradually settling down. Several thousand British officers here now.[5] They are coming from various camps. We were the first lot in; the camp is vast but very poorly equipped for room space and facilities, etc.

One third of a Canadian Red Cross parcel was issued to us this evening. First square meal for months! What an enormous treat. Everyone more cheerful but anxious for the other two thirds! Have met several friends here, Kenneth Dee, etc. Have started smoking my pipe again, thanks to the generosity of others.

All the officers caught in 1940 are here and they seem to have masses of everything and are being very kind indeed to us.

Am sorry to say that I am now separated from Jack, as all majors are put together. I have often wondered how such a professorial type as Jack Hamson could have become a 'cloak and dagger' merchant. One day he was enlightening me in the best way to cut someone's throat, and the most effective way to use knuckledusters, and I asked him where on earth he had acquired this knowledge, to which he replied 'I went on a course!' He has it in mind to write a book about his adventures, which he is going to call, 'A Day in the Life of a Don'!

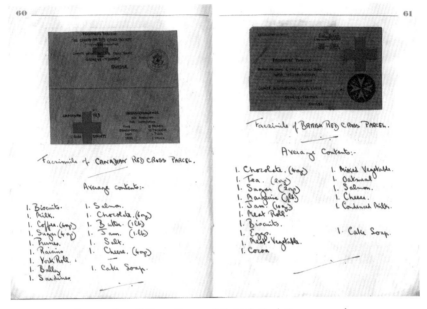

Facsimiles of Canadian and British Red Cross parcels.

<u>15th October 1941</u>

Have been appointed ADC and interpreter to General Kaffatos. Here in this enormous camp it is very necessary for him to have someone to help him and as my Greek is now pretty good the choice fell to me pretty naturally. However, it is the luckiest chance for me because I can be really useful and I have the greatest respect for the old man. I now share a small room for two with him, Room No. 4 in Block 7, and we are very comfortable. General V. M. Fortune,[6] CB, DSO, the Senior British prisoner in Germany, is now Senior British Officer here and had a very nice interview with him.

We were issued with a further one-third parcel today. Also today, the representative of the International Red Cross visited and was horrified by conditions here.[7] The lights failed tonight and I used my improvised boot-polish lamp, which is very efficient.

<u>16th October 1941</u>

Full British Red Cross parcel issued to us today and we are really beginning to appease our hunger. Saw Dr Odell, RAMC, about my hernia, which he confirms, and I am to see him again later when the camp is more settled. It does not give me a great deal of pain; I have to remember about weights and strain.

Weather very cold and wet and muddy. Have met many friends here among almost three thousand officers. There are thirty-five Old Harrovians – many of them my contemporaries.

<u>18th October 1941</u>

Excellent concert given by officers from the other parts of the camp this afternoon. Weather continues bad. Hunger slightly appeased. Find I need to visit the lavatory almost every day now instead of once every four days as previously.

<u>21st October 1941</u>

Food plentiful now thanks to parcels and great generosity to General Kaffatos and myself by other officers. The German authorities have imposed reprisals. We are not allowed out of our huts after 7.00 pm because it is alleged that POW camps in Canada for German POWs are under the same conditions.

<u>23rd October 1941</u>

Have been appointed 'checker' of parcels from the store. The General and I are in the RAF battalion, as our little room happens to be in their block. Very refreshing to be with all these young fellows, who are incredibly kind and polite and considerate to my General. Camp gradually settling down but latrines and washhouses are indescribably filthy as they cannot possibly cope with the numbers in the camp. Am very fortunate to be in a small room where one can heat water for washing on our little stove. Every night we have a brew and chat in one or other of the fifteen rooms in our hut and life is very social. We have lectures in the evening and I have re-given the Cretan lectures, which were much appreciated. The medical authorities are very worried about the state of health of the officers who came through Salonika, and we are being issued with an extra invalid parcel per week for a month. The General and I are reasonably fit but some are still suffering considerably from dysentery. Actually, the trouble is the conditions at Salonika followed by those at Lübeck. Am now the only army officer on parade in our battalion, which is entirely RN, RM, and RAF. General Kaffatos does not come on parade but is counted in his room. Today a tunnel was found and three RAF officers are in the 'cooler'.[8]

30th October 1941
First heavy fall of snow – winter has come. Am still in summer khakis. Camp settling down well and am comparatively happy.

31st October 1941
Received further letters. General Kaffatos and I are preparing two further lectures on Crete (by request) for the whole camp this time. Went to a show of Highland dancing this afternoon. Had letters from Tony and Carl.[9]

4th November 1941
Had my first shower (cold!) for a month! But can always get a good all-over wash in the room. Thick snow and ice. Had tea yesterday with Brigadier Parrington. Am much less food conscious these days and visibly gaining weight. My hernia troubles me a bit and I shall have to see the Medical Officer again.

9th November 1941
Cinema show on 7th and an officers' variety show yesterday. Weather still cold but slushy. Saw Medical Officer today about my hernia and he advised an operation in England after the war and no truss now, unless it gets worse. Ian Fernie (Royal Tank Regiment) is here and see quite a lot of him – we give him our extra coal as our stove is a very small one.

12th November 1941
Turkish Red Crescent have sent some bulk food to the camp, dried fruits, sardines, sweets, etc. – very welcome. Gave the two lectures on Crete on 10th and today: seemed to go down alright. General Fortune was there on both occasions.

16th November 1941
Invited Brigadier Parrington and Captain Clark-Hall RN to tea. Weather now warm and fine. Another tunnel was found yesterday.

17th November 1941
Room 4 in our block had a little concert last night – very good show. The star turn was Sgt Slattery, RAF, the first British prisoner of war shot down at Kiel on 4th September 1939.[10]

18th November 1941
The representatives of the Protecting Power[11] are expected tomorrow and General Kaffatos has an interview with them. America acts for us.

19th November 1941
Attended the interview with the Americans as interpreter to General Kaffatos. They say they feel sure they can get him sent back to Crete, as he is the only Greek officer prisoner in Germany and should not be with British officers. But will America be involved in the war before negotiations are completed? Knox and Wood, the Americans, are very kind.

25th November 1941
Three hundred Russian prisoners of war are reputed to be in an adjoining camp to this one, but out of sight from us.[12]

26th November 1941
Medical Officer now advises a truss and I was measured for mine today, during the course of which operation they discovered that I was also ruptured on the right side – so the belt will have to be a double one.

27th November 1941
Trouble over parcels. Germans now want to open every tin. Sanitary conditions still shockingly bad. Admitted to be so by the Germans themselves.

30th November 1941
There was a soccer match today – England and Scotland. England won three–two. The teams were composed of orderlies.

1st December 1941
Six months captured today. Weather very cold – nineteen and half degrees of frost F[13] on parade this morning at 9.00 am.

Fuck Hitler.
Surrounded by spindles for winding flax or wool, the warring nations are
represented by the British lion, Russian hammer and sickle, German swastika
and the Italian eagle. In the outer border, 'FUCKHITLER' is written four
and a half times in Morse Code; in the inner, 'GODSAVETHEKING' appears
three times. The embroidery hung on various prison walls. The Germans never
noticed the insult. 410 x 492 mm

2nd December 1941

Still bitterly cold, seventeen degrees of frost F. Russians are in the top camp and are apparently being extremely badly treated. I still have no jacket and it is pretty chilly.

4th December 1941

There was a stay-in strike today. All those without minimum clothing requirements stayed off parade, fifty-four out of one hundred and sixty-one in our battalion. I doubt if it will have any effect. Had today my first letter from Mother.

8th December 1941

Rumours of a move! Repeated visits by Red Cross, American and high German officials have declared that this camp is a disgrace. Nous verrons![14] Collection made for the Russians, thirty thousand cigarettes: everyone gave willingly as their lot is so much worse than ours.

9th December 1941

Fateful day: Japan and America in the war – when will it all end now?[15] Squadron Leader Murray[16] has given me a piece of canvas and I am doing a bit of work with some wool from General Kaffatos's pullover. It passes the time wonderfully.[17]

13th December 1941

Big search today following attempted escape. There were some ugly scenes. Colonel Goodwin was hit twice with a rifle in the face (black eye and lost a tooth) – several officers in our battalion kicked by the German guards. An enormous quantity of food and clothing was damaged – one might almost say wilfully. Our room looked as though a tornado had swept through it, but not much material damage.

16th December 1941

Received my first excellent parcel from Egypt. Weather very wet. No news of my truss yet. Senior Medical Officer reckons it will be a case of operation and then three months' rest.

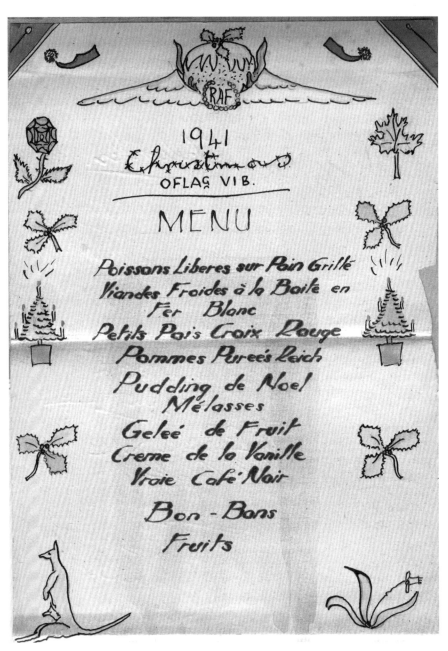

Christmas Menu, 1941.
The French translates as 'Free grilled fish, cold tinned meat in white fat,
Red Cross peas, Reich mashed potato, Christmas pudding, molasses, fruit jelly,
vanilla custard, real black coffee, sweets and fruit'.

7. CHRISTMAS 1941

20th December 1941

Carol service – very impressive. Still very wet. Strong rumour two hundred and fifty officers are moving. General Kaffatos and I are not on the list. The move is doubtless due to the countless reports that this camp is a disgrace.

22nd December 1941

Heavy frost last night. Not likely to get any clothes here: all are too small.

25th December 1941

What a Xmas! Seventy-five per cent of our battalion drunk on homemade brew.[1] I had some but not too much! In the evening, General Kaffatos and I dined in Room 4: we had all saved up food and our small room was used as the kitchen. Really excellent show. Tony Trumble (Wing Commander, DFC), the hut commander, presided. Again, General Kaffatos and I were the only army officers – we were about twenty. After dinner the rowdiness started. We kept out of it. It was chiefly 'fighter' versus 'bomber'! Bottles, plates, doors smashed, an absolute shambles! No one hurt luckily. There are bound to be repercussions about the drunks on evening parade. What a day! Three in our hut were too drunk to get out of bed. Felt really happy today.

26th December 1941

Weather extremely cold – snow and frost. My moustache iced up on parade. My boots were frozen to the floor in our room. Our Battalion Commander (Commander Beale, Fleet Air Arm) has been sacked for the Xmas Day affair! We hear the SBO takes a dim view of it too! I would not have missed it for anything. Did me a power of good!

29th December 1941

Big raid last night – lasted on and off from 10.00 pm to 7.00 am. Terribly cold – everything frozen up in the room (which has three outside wooden walls!) as soon as the stove goes out, one blanket and a greatcoat is not enough. The Russians here are in a terrible state – many of the poor wretches have died.[2] They are just skin and bone – we see them being deloused.

30th December 1941

Twenty-nine degrees of frost F this morning. Issued today with a blanket

Col. (temp.) F. G. A. Smyth, C.B.E. (8763).
Col. (Bt.) H. V. Walsh, T.D. (24277).
Lt.-Col. R. McKinlay (8719).
Lt.-Col. W. Russell (15662).
Lt.-Col. A. Swindale (28990).
Maj. (temp. Lt.-Col.) G. A. E. Argo, O.B.E., M.C. (50524).
Maj. (temp. Lt.-Col.) P. J. L. Capon (39084).
Maj. (temp. Lt.-Col.) R. K. Debenham (89075).
Maj. (temp. Lt.-Col.) F. A. R. Hacker (10652).
Maj. (temp. Lt.-Col.) W. D. Hughes (40252).
Maj. (temp. Lt.-Col.) C. B. Levick (96417).
Maj. (temp. Lt.-Col.) P. Lloyd-Williams, T.D. (7544).
Maj. (actg. Lt.-Col.) A. N. B. Odbert (42438).
Capt. (actg. Lt.-Col.) H. A. Crouch, O.B.E., M.C. (8653) (Res. of Off.).
Maj. C. R. Croft (42311).
Maj. J. B. S. Guy (40285).
Maj. W. H. Milligan (88876).
Capt. (temp. Maj.) J. M. Black (95879).
Capt. (temp. Maj.) J. W. Crofton (89807).
Capt. (temp. Maj.) A. H. T. F. Fullerton (65324).
Capt. (temp. Maj.) P. D. C. Kinmont (87341).
Capt. (temp. Maj.) W. G. MacFie (75591).
Capt. (temp. Maj.) M. M. Medine (75594).
Capt. (temp. Maj.) E. F. S. Morrison (62831).
Capt. (temp. Maj.) H. N. Perkins (66484).
Capt. (temp. Maj.) R. A. Smart (70117).
Capt. (temp. Maj.) R. A. Stephen (63177).
Capt. (temp. Maj.) S. M. Vassallo (102686).
Capt. (actg. Maj.) J. M. Corall (73583).
Capt. (actg. Maj.) R. D. Holloway (87776).
Capt. (actg. Maj.) A. C. Rumsey (106812).
Capt. (actg. Maj.) J. P. Springett (39610).
Lt. (Qr.-Mr.) (local Maj.) S. W. Hobday (71262).
Capt. L. V. Arundell (99687).
Capt. F. B. Brown (122718).
Capt. A. G. Carmichael (87860).
Capt. N. F. Coghill (114203).
Capt. A. J. Daly (112408).
Capt. R. T. Fletcher (119618).
Capt. W. G. France (92491).
Capt. R. P. Hendry (73575).
Capt. R. P. Lawson (115755).
Capt. J. H. B. Livingston (42478).
Capt. H. J. McCann (89979).
Capt. R. J. Niven (70118).
Capt. M. G. Pearson (108695).
Capt. E. J. Richardson (78550).
Capt. J. W. Spence (102683).
Capt. J. A. G. Wilson (85206).
7258757 W.O. I (R.S.M.) G. L. Williams.
7458858 W.O. II (actg. W.O. I) W. R. Beattie.
7257290 W.O. II (actg. W.O. I) G. B. Martin.
7255354 S.-Sergt. (actg. W.O. I (S.S.M.)) G. H. Dugmore.
7258506 W.O. II J. V. Hutchinson.
7345861 W.O. II (Q.M.S.) J. D. Whittaker.
7358640 S.-Sergt. W. Geddes.
7258707 S.-Sergt. J. Harford.
7259337 S.-Sergt. J. W. B. Hughes.
7250150 S.-Sergt. E. Mackie.
7260580 S.-Sergt. W. J. Regan.
7262546 Sergt. K. A. Barker.
7339939 Sergt. W. Barrow.
7345985 Sergt. A. R. D. Jones.
7347353 Sergt. T. Kay.
7259634 Sergt. F. J. Knightly.
7261085 Sergt. K. W. Lyons.
7517214 Corpl. (actg. Sergt.) J. C. Davis.
7260747 Corpl. (actg. Sergt.) E. J. Ireland.
7516767 Corpl. (actg. Sergt.) G. Masters.
7263776 Pte. (actg. Sergt.) P. C. Gavin.

7263232 Corpl. W. H. Bissell.
7632149 Corpl. A. N. Cotton.
2752294 Corpl. F. M. Currie.
4684768 Corpl. C. Dodsworth.
7263037 Corpl. G. H. Fellows.
7263567 Corpl. W. Hutcheson.
7349251 Corpl. F. G. Page.
7262205 Corpl. D. Smith.
7368467 Pte. (actg. Corpl.) T. C. Bell.
7381979 Pte. (actg. Corpl.) L. J. H. Gibson.
7263560 Pte. (actg. Corpl.) J. J. Simpson.
7263098 Lce.-Corpl. W. Bolton.
7262998 Lce.-Corpl. G. F. Coates.
7265341 Pte. H. W. Bown.
7373315 Pte. F. Chapman.
7263415 Pte. J. Crozier.
7535006 Pte. L. Farrar.
7365581 Pte. L. P. Munns.
7516827 Pte. R. Riddell.
7382075 Pte. J. D. Smith.
7264061 Pte. T. Smith.

ROYAL ARMY ORDNANCE CORPS.

Brig. (actg.) W. W. Richards, C.B.E., M.C. (14698).
Col. C. F. Douglas-White, O.B.E. (9432).
Col. (temp.) J. C. Connan, O.B.E. (191241).
Col. (temp.) J. W. Gaisford (8903).
Lt.-Col. W. D. Gundel, D.C.M. (31808).
Lt.-Col. G. C. Shaw (4139).
Maj. (temp. Lt.-Col.) H. S. Baker (52740).
Maj. (temp. Lt.-Col.) N. Berry (52300).
Maj. (temp. Lt.-Col.) S. F. Clark (100815).
Maj. (temp. Lt.-Col.) B. G. Cox (13142).
Maj. (temp. Lt.-Col.) H. H. Fitton (18300).
Maj. (temp. Lt.-Col.) E. J. Kinvig (66408).
Maj. (temp. Lt.-Col.) W. S. Mackay (111751).
Maj. (temp. Lt.-Col.) H. F. Mackenzie, M.B.E. (40619).
Maj. (temp. Lt.-Col.) E. B. Stewart-Smith (103311).
Maj. (actg. Lt.-Col.) D. A. K. Redman (173375).
Maj. G. S. McKellar (47267).
Maj. R. B. Winton (73744).
Maj. (Qr.-Mr.) A. MacKay (112434).
Capt. (temp. Maj.) W. J. Austin (165478).
Capt. (temp. Maj.) W. P. Dixon (44847).
Capt. (temp. Maj.) R. H. Ferguson (111241).
Capt. (temp. Maj.) R. H. Groombridge (106608).
Capt. (temp. Maj.) P. J. Grover (106348).
Capt. (temp. Maj.) N. M. Harris (67494).
Capt. (temp. Maj.) A. A. Jarvis (98686).
Capt. (temp. Maj.) F. L. Manning (118038).
Capt. (temp. Maj.) S. K. Neill (107698).
Capt. (temp. Maj.) E. C. Nicholls (49891).
Capt. (temp. Maj.) C. I. E. Rabagliati (64809).
Capt. (temp. Maj.) D. J. C. Robertson (71471).
Capt. (temp. Maj.) C. Sellars (98772).
Capt. (temp. Maj.) H. Shore (52323).
Capt. (actg. Maj.) G. C. Drake-Brockman (34231).
Capt. (actg. Maj.) A. W. T. Weir (45175).
Lt. (actg. Maj.) C. P. Brady (104875).
Lt. (actg. Maj.) A. T. Casdagli (108542).
Lt. (actg. Maj.) A. Kenyon (115446).
Lt. (actg. Maj.) W. A. Paston (86338).
Lt. (actg. Maj.) T. A. Perry (55956).
2nd Lt. (actg. Maj.) P. E. Goodall (130465).
Lt. (temp. Capt.) E. A. Catesby (99688).
Lt. (temp. Capt.) M. C. Clear (88428).
Lt. (temp. Capt.) J. A. Davies (94785).
Lt. (temp. Capt.) W. K. Ford (107333).
Lt. (temp. Capt.) B. Gaccon (106661).
Lt. (temp. Capt.) T. A. B. Gemmel (106621).

Casdagli Mentioned in Despatches for distinguished service:
The London Gazette, 26 December 1941, No 35396. A bronze
oak leaf is the emblem of this honour.

from the Red Cross but cannot get a jacket. No news of the truss yet.

1st January 1942
Pantomime, 'Citronella', last night – excellent show. We had a really splendid musical evening in our hut and I bought the New Year in. A heavy thaw has set in.

5th January 1942
Mud inches-deep all over the camp. This is a real trial as the rooms get filthy and in the dark one can only walk outside with the greatest danger of falling into a deep pothole – my jackboots are very useful. The latest order is that we cannot write to or receive letters from occupied countries – not quite according to the Convention! This cuts me off from Menda.

8th January 1942
Hard frost again. My truss has arrived and cost me forty-five marks (three pounds) and seems a pretty solid affair.[3] Not too uncomfortable. Have heard General Kaffatos and I are to move from here on January 15th to Spangenberg, Oflag IX-A/H, with about two hundred others – all senior officers. Another move![4] What chances of any private parcels now?

9th January 1942
Went to the pantomime again today as guests of General Fortune, together with Brigadiers Somerset and Nicholson.[5]

13th January 1942
Still very hard frost. Neither General Kaffatos nor I wish to move and have tried hard to get out of it. It is most refreshing being with all these young fellows. They have the real spirit and outlook on life.

14th January 1942
Borrowed some skates and did a few rounds of the homemade rink.[6] Had a farewell tea with Ken Dee – am very sorry indeed to be moving.

15th January 1942
Last night General Kaffatos went into every room in the block to say his personal goodbyes. He is very popular in spite of knowing no English – personality counts for a lot. Reveille[7] at 2.30 am. Search at 4.00 am. Left camp at 6.15 am. Arrived at Dössel station at 8.00 am. Train did not leave till 11.45 am. Frightfully cold.

OFLAG IX-A/H, SPANGENBERG

Oflag IX-A/H, Spangenberg, was made up of the Lower Camp in the village of Elbersdorf and the Upper Camp, less than half a mile away, a medieval moated castle on top of a rocky hill. It first opened in October 1939 as Oflag IX-A for RAF and Armée de l'Air POWs. In June 1940, it was renamed Oflag IX-A/H. Virtually no communication was allowed between camps.

The Sam Browne belt.

8. THIS YEAR, NEXT YEAR, SOMETIME...

15th January 1942
Arrived at Oflag IX-A/H, Spangenberg, at 4.00 pm travelling via Hümme, Hofgeismar, Malsfeld, Kassel and Elbersdorf.[1] Spent the night at the Lower Camp in the village. General Kaffatos went direct to the Top Camp. First impressions are good except for the terrible cold: could get no sleep.

16th January 1942
Left at 8.30 am for the Castle. Arrived at 9.00 am and was again searched – getting quite used to it now. Found that the steep climb had affected General Kaffatos on the previous day and he had passed out. He is better today. We have been allotted a small room for two but it has one great disadvantage in that we have to pass through two other rooms to get in or out! The Castle is about twelve hundred feet up and perishing cold. The general impression is that the move is for the worse – but things may improve – nous verrons.

17th January 1942
Very little food. One-seventh of a loaf and we are back to starvation diet until the heavy baggage arrives with our food. A very minute search carried out here, my Sam Browne belt was confiscated! Weather continues bitterly cold.

23rd January 1942
Twenty-five to thirty degrees of frost F every morning and fifteen to twenty degrees in the afternoons. Things are a little better. Bulk Red Cross food has been issued. German rations very poor. Still one-seventh loaf bread. Our room is comfortable but very small. We are two hundred and ten here now. General Kaffatos and I are in a mess of ten with Lt Colonels Page, Wright, Hamilton, Pope, Gethin, Clay, Adams and Major Clark: all caught in 1940. They are very kind to us.

27th January 1942
No parcels have arrived yet. We are very hungry now. Record low temperature here of thirty-four degrees of frost F. Inspected by German Gen. in charge of the Kassel area. Put before him the case of General Kaffatos but little hope now of him being sent back to Greece. Went to the Medical Officer (Captain James, RAMC) about my rupture but he says no chance of being operated on here: my truss fits well but I must not strain myself.

Photograph stamped *'Kriegsgefangener'*,
German for 'Prisoner of War'.

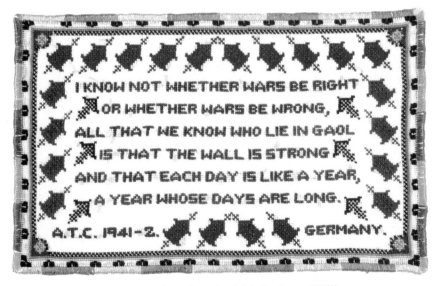

The Ballad of Reading Gaol (1). By Oscar Wilde.
Casdagli changes 'laws' is changed to 'wars'. 407 x 240 mm

<u>3rd February 1942</u>

Had some letters today, also a games parcel! Life much the same – very dull. Am reading the 'Herries Chronicle'[2] – am well steeped in it.

<u>9th February 1942</u>

Finished 'Herries Chronicle'. Photograph taken yesterday by the Germans for identification purposes.

    Big search of rooms today. Weather warmer but everything is still white. We have a nice little stove in our room.

<u>12th February 1942</u>

I am now the recognised authority on embroidery! Gave lessons today to Brigadier Eden and Brigadier Somerset. Am working quite hard at it.[3]

<u>17th February 1942</u>

More snow and therefore weather not so cold. Have just finished reading the 'Iliad' – grand stuff.[4] My rupture, in spite of the truss, gets no better but then I do not suppose it is likely to: the bulge seems rather bigger if anything.

<u>21st February 1942</u>

Did a little sawing and chopping wood today as we have not enough coal for our weekly shower. Our laundry is sent to the village and dealt with by the local women: it all depends upon what sort of frau you get. Both times I have had bad fraus,[5] blast them! All buttons broken, etc.

<u>25th February 1942</u>

More rumours of moves have been current and came to a head today and eight officers have left for the Bottom Camp, including the other eight members of our mess! Thirty-five RAF officers are coming here to the Top Camp.

<u>26th February 1942</u>

The RAF have arrived and General Kaffatos and I are in a new mess, mostly officers we know who were caught in Crete – Dick Boileau, Ken Hardie, etc. The camp will now be less crowded. Had a note from Roger Elletson who is now at the Lower Camp after staying in Belgrade for quite a time in hospital.

<u>4th March 1942</u>

Swiss Commission[6] arrived today. Interviewed them with General Kaffatos. He stated his case and hopes something can be done. The Swiss have taken over from the Americans. His case is that he is a Greek officer and should

Map of Crete. 250 x 150 mm

therefore be among his own nationality – incidentally, he knows that all his comrades have been released! Weather colder again and thick snow.

11th March 1942

Another Swiss Commission from Geneva visited the camp yesterday. Coal has now run out and we are given a little wood which we cut ourselves: did a little sawing and yesterday peeled potatoes for five hours as we are very short of orderlies. At last, after nine months, I have got a battle dress blouse. I feel overdressed! My shoes are very bad now and the German boots leak and are very uncomfortable. YMCA Commission[7] came today about boots and games and educational facilities. The thaw has set in; there is so much mud about that with leaky shoes it is not worth going out. Our total exercise space is the outer battlement, some sixty yards long, even then only at special times. Repeated requests for walks have not yet borne fruit.

21st March 1942

Twelve Greek officers from Crete have arrived and my time is full as interpreter and 'liaison' officer. No one, not even the Germans, knows why they are in Germany – much less here. They are all junior ranks and some of them very old and others very young. Only one regular among them. They are in Room 17. Today finished my embroidery of a map of Crete, which I have made out of some of the coloured threads from General Kaffatos's pyjamas! There are about forty-five thousand stitches and it took me about one hundred and ninety hours – the stitches are pretty fine.

31st March 1942

Had some more letters from Cairo. I have roughly thirty-five hundred pounds sterling at the office, thirteen hundred at Barclays, three hundred and seventy-five pounds sterling in England, three hundred pounds sterling which Theo owes me and about fifteen hundred pounds value of shares in Cairo.[8] Have been busy building seats round the Castle with Bertie MacLeay (Camerons). Have temporarily stopped embroidery owing to lack of materials.

1st April 1942

Concert last night, quite amusing but not much talent. Now very short of food and smokes. Only three fifths of a Red Cross parcel since 19th March.

7th April 1942

Letters from home advise me of twelve tobacco parcels and three personal ones – but NOTHING arrived yet. Am working on a bookmark in petit

CORRESPONDENCE

We are grateful to Mrs. Pope for the opportunit: of publishing the following extracts from letters written by her son, A. L. Pope, The Knoll (1926²), from the Prisoner of War Camp Oflag IX A in May and June, 1941.

"Have founded Harrow Association Oflag IX A, and have played and beaten Eton at cricket in spite of fact Vice-Captain only one eye, and two of side only one leg! Also beat them at darts and tiddley-winks—suggest Lord's takes place here after the war. . . ."

"We have initiated a magnificent game of prison cricket. The ball is made out of all sorts of oddments bound round firmly with elastoplast; the bat is a masterpiece of *Gefangener* inventiveness, and wickets and bails such as you would pay half a guinea for. We have worked out an elaborate system of boundaries, out of the camp being 6-and-out. We've played two matches so far, and have nets in evening! Changing-room is pavilion and we have two umpires and a scorer, and give colours and have seats in the pav. All these details are so exact that really one gets the feeling of cricket: in fact, in the last match, my side versus the doctor's side—stake two barrels of beer—the doctor's side won by one run. For five hours we all forgot about our fate. The village seemed to be very interested, except possibly the German guards who spent most of their time fishing the ball out of the stream. Yes, it's a very cheery camp, and everyone sees the best side always. That's the best asset in a camp."

It appears that parcels and letters are getting through fairly regularly, and the writer says that letters are "almost as welcome as parcels."

POST SCRIPT

Salvage is a co---

From *The Harrovian*, 28 January 1942.

point.[9] Am now quite used to my truss. I still maintain that I should not tell Joyce or the family – I think I am right.

10th April 1942
My birthday![10] German rations have been cut down since 6th April and we now only get two thousand grams of bread per week, three hundred grams of meat, etc. Since we have had no parcels since 19th March I am absolutely ravenous again, tobacco also at a premium. Surprise birthday present today from Egypt. Parcel with slippers, cottons, etc.

16th April 1942
Swiss Legation[11] arrived today. Was present at their interview with the Greek officers; they say they will do what they can for them.[12] Some Red Cross parcels have arrived – enough for two weeks. The names of the Swiss were Nivella and Malinguist. Have made quite a nice stick out of a bit of spruce. Warmer weather but cold wind. Travelling cinema on Saturday – not a bad film – English subtitles.

17th April 1942
This camp is certainly subjected to the most frequent searches – every few days the tornado descends. We were visited today for about half an hour by three searchers. Searches can be of any type – from just a cursory look round to the strip variety where even the anus and private parts are closely examined. Dignified treatment for senior British officers – but one must keep a sense of humour. It certainly helps one and simply infuriates the Germans.

21st April 1942
Stump cricket[13] has started in the moat. Played today for the Army versus RAF – we were beaten. Warmer weather. Among the RAF is Aidan Crawley[14] who had also been for a few days at Salonika.

25th April 1942
Anzac Day.[15] Played for England versus Anzacs – beat them by an innings. Two tobacco parcels arrived today – wonderfully welcome they were too.

26th April 1942
We are now allowed once every fourteen days to walk on parole[16] to the village sports ground. Went on 24th and enjoyed it – nice walk, kicked a football about and collected some dandelions for salad! Have now got a pair of boots from the Red Cross, which is one thing less to worry about.

Parole card, Oflag IX-A/H.

O Jupiter.
50 x 320 mm

<u>28th April 1942</u>

The forty-six RAF officers who were here have now been moved to another camp – very sorry to see them go – our numbers down to about one hundred and fifty now.

<u>2nd May 1942</u>

Weather colder again; snow yesterday and thick snow this morning – melting rapidly of course. For the last few days I have been working hard in the moat digging, etc., morning and afternoon.[17] My truss is a little uncomfortable but otherwise no ill effects. I must take some exercise anyway. There seems to be no hope of having an operation done in Germany.

<u>8th May 1942</u>

Warmer weather and I work in the moat nearly all day now, digging and shifting stones and trying to get the place shipshape. It may not be the best thing for my rupture but the time simply flies, and the moat is looking a different place now.

I had today my first parcel from Turkey, from Jack Hamson's mother[18] – God bless her!

<u>18th May 1942</u>

Life goes on: plenty of work in the moat. Stump cricket in the afternoons. Weather warm.

Got my fountain pen back which was confiscated at Lübeck – wonders will never cease.

No news from Menda for some time. Had a parcel with clothes from Cairo – it arrived in just four weeks! No personal parcels at all from Joyce yet.

<u>22nd May 1942</u>

Eight more officers have arrived from the Lower Camp and brought me news of Roger.[19] We are back to about one hundred and eighty here now.

<u>23rd May 1942</u>

Played roulette[20] this evening and backed 'ten' being Tony's coming birthday. I made seventy marks[21] – it came up three times out of forty-nine.

<u>24th May 1942</u>

Two officers escaped from the Lower Camp, Peter Dollar (Fourth Hussars) and Dick Lorraine (RE) whom I have not seen since Salonika. They were caught this morning.

26th May 1942
Work all morning in the moat. Usually cricket in the afternoon; reading, embroidery and other pursuits help to pass the evenings. We have two parades and are counted twice in our rooms during the night. German rationing from bad to worse. It is only thanks to the Red Cross parcels that we exist at all – at least in moderate health.

28th May 1942
One of the Cretan officers, Theodosiades, is due to be sent to Belgrade and then to be repatriated to his home.[22] He leaves on Monday. What astonishing people the Germans are!

31st May 1942
Weather improving. Gardening. Gardens growing. Still embroidering.

1st June 1942
In the bag a year today.[23] Theodosiades left today taking with him three tablets of soap and six bars of chocolate for Menda in Athens. I only hope he can get it through.

As it is now exactly a year since I was captured, now at Spangenberg Castle in Germany I intend to write as nearly as I can remember the incidents during my last few days of freedom and my first few days as a prisoner. There are many reasons why I have decided to do this. Firstly, in years to come, it may be of interest to Tony's grandchildren and it will even be interesting to Tony himself, I hope. Secondly, well-remembered facts are becoming less clear in my memory and, before fancy and imagination take too firm a hold, I want to get down on paper the true facts, a story which no one but myself can write. Thirdly, because to my astonishment the Germans returned my fountain pen to me the other day, having had it for nearly a year! These seem to me to be good reasons for embarking on that rather sad story.[24]

4th June 1942
Went with General Kaffatos to the dentist – lovely walk through the village.

5th June 1942
Camp inspected by new German General of the district. International Committee arrived in the evening to board people for repatriation.[25]

9th June 1942
Played for the Ex-Kreta XI versus St Valery Harriers. We won easily. I

distinguished myself by breaking the first window of the season, and this scoring twelve! This is the sort of cricket in which I regularly get to bowl. My shorts were returned today.

16th June 1942
We have had a week of rain now, very cold. Had another parcel from Turkey.

18th June 1942
A stranger to me, Jules Dierckx of 136, West 16th Street, New York, USA, has sent me a magnificent food parcel from America. Extraordinary business!

19th June 1942
Received a parcel of a pillow from Mrs Campbell in Portugal!

25th June 1942
We are now used to the news that Tobruk has fallen and that the enemy are in Egypt.[26] It is a sad blow, as this will delay the day of victory. Getting out of this place is all one ever dreams of.

Went again to the dentist with General Kaffatos. He has had five teeth out and still another two to come! Poor chap – he is taking it well.

26th June 1942
Fine spell has broken, terrific storm last night.

27th June 1942
Twelve officers from the St Nazaire Raid[27] have arrived here – everyone very pleased to see new faces in the camp and particularly fresh young blood.

4th July 1942
Events in Egypt are worrying, still one can do nothing from here – just hope for the best.

Germans have cut the coal ration by fifty per cent. Little hot water available and only one hot meal a day. Weather better again.

7th July 1942
Big day today – my first parcel from Joyce arrived and what a magnificent one too – everything quite superlative – have waited thirteen months for it!

8th July 1942
Inoculated today against typhoid. Am very smart in all my new clothes.

The battlements of the east bastion, Oflag IX-A/H.

Two prisoners seem dressed as Roman women,
possibly Portia and Calpurnia, the only two female
characters, in *Julius Caesar*.

17th July 1942

Have now finished visits to the dentist; all the old man's teeth are now out. He will go to a hospital soon for a plate. I have some holes in my teeth but shall wait till I get home. This man is a botcher – I have seen enough of him. My rupture is under control, although it hurts at times; I probably should not play so much cricket – but I shall!

Two days ago we had an Art and Craft Exhibition. I organised the tapestry side. Great success. I showed six pieces. Weather wet and cold again. What a truly horrible country this is.

18th July 1942

Big day today because I have heard from Tony[28] in Athens that Theodosiades had arrived and delivered the chocolate and soap. It must be the only case of a prisoner of war sending food to someone else outside the camp! Everyone was very interested and happy it got through.

24th July 1942

Gave a lecture to Agricultural Society on 'Cotton Growing'. Remarkable how much detail came back with really very little effort. I continue next Friday.

25th July 1942

I acted in the variety show in a 'cricket sketch' – quite amusing, went down well. Weather fine today after weeks of rain. My chief activities now are teaching Greek to the English, teaching English to the Greeks, embroidery, cricket, keeping the cricket ground in order, reading and being ADC to General Kaffatos, being liaison officer to the Greeks, apart from other 'duties'. The days pass but it is a long tedious drag.

1st August 1942

'Julius Caesar' presented in the courtyard by the officers. Very good show. Well acted and well produced; all the clothes came from Kassel.

5th August 1942

Five officers left today for Dössel. Also comes the news that the Greek officers including General Kaffatos are to be moved from this camp in a day or two. Secondly, we are no longer allowed to write home or receive letters from home until the proportion of letters received by German prisoners of war in Australia is known! We shall then be based on the same monthly proportion. This applies all over Germany to British prisoners and they will be based on letters received by Germans in the Empire. This camp has been specially

ΣΟΛΩΝ ΚΑΦΦΑΤΟΣ
ΕΚ ΡΕΘΥΜΝΗΣ
ΑΝΤΙΣΤΡΑΤΗΓΟΣ

General Solon Kaffatos, Companion of the Order of the Bath,
French Croix de Guerre, Serbian Croix de Guerre and the
Greek Military Medal (twice).

selected to be based on Australia but, knowing how few letters the Australians here are getting from their families, we are not at all hopeful.

6th August 1942
Greek officers left today and General Kaffatos joins them tomorrow at 2.45 am. Everyone is very sorry they are leaving. They go to Biberach.[29] General Fortune sent for me and thanked me for the way I had looked after the old man and told me how it had been noticed by everyone. 'A difficult job well done' was the way he put it. To me it was a pleasure in any case.

7th August 1942
General Kaffatos left at 2.45 am and this breaks another link in the chain. We have been fourteen months together and I have nothing but the very greatest respect and liking for him. We shall meet again one day, I shall see to that. He was a real soldier of the best type.

10th August 1942
Am alone in our little room now. I expect I shall have to move into a big room soon. Several rooms are being whitewashed. Yesterday the Highland Brigade were out for 0 against the orderlies! Last night we had prunes; it was arranged by our PMC,[30] without us knowing, that the stones should work out at 'this year' but we got the wrong bowl from the kitchen and we all had 'never'.[31]

17th August 1942
Am still alone in my room, in perfect comfort and peace. I shall be moved any day now. I miss General Kaffatos a lot. We have been a long, happy time together and, incidentally, he was one of the nicest men I've ever met.

Map of England. 350 x 460 mm

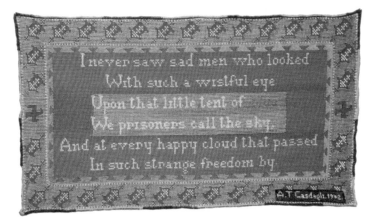

The Ballad of Reading Gaol (2). 340 x 210 mm

9. THE STRANGE FREEDOM OF CLOUDS

18th August 1942
Today moved to my new room, No. 13, with nine other majors. They are all friends of mine and I am very lucky; all of them caught in France in 1940. Among them are Hill (exciseman),[1] MacLeay (taxidermist), Fenely (lawyer), Johnson (retired Indian Army), Gee (housemaster at Clifton),[2] Christopherson (Lloyds).[3]

24th August 1942
Two officers escaped yesterday but were re-caught. Both were doctors, named Stoker and Hetherington. They were beaten up when caught and Stoker is in hospital with a fractured skull. Actually, the butt of a rifle was BROKEN over his head after he had given himself up. Reprisals are being taken against this particular camp over mail.[4] All other camps in Germany are now having their mail; our mail is being held up both in and out – the only camp in Germany. They have been playing this game on us for a month now.

28th August 1942
Big raid last night. Stoker is better; the Germans say their soldier will be punished.

3rd September 1942
Three years of war today. The ban on letters is still on. Am taking part in a skit on 'Julius Caesar' called 'Scarlet Cinna'; written by Rupert Christie and very witty. Since 18th August I have been working on an embroidered map of England, drawn for me by Major Shears, RE of Hutchinsons, the publishers. The local threshing machine in the village is working solidly from 6.00 am to 11.40 pm. Beautiful weather.

8th September 1942
'Scarlet Cinna' went off very well on 5th and 7th. My part consisted, among other things, of singing three songs[5] and appearing in one scene as an ancient Briton prisoner of war and in another as a Vestal Virgin! The rest of the cast, except for Rupert and me, was composed of the St Nazaire crowd – really good fun.

9th September 1942
Still no news re letters. Weather getting colder.

<u>15th September 1942</u>
We have now heard that the Germans are continuing their reprisals on letters and that we shall have no letters in or out for at least another month – what a nation! An attempted escape on Sunday has put our hosts on their toes! Received a uniform parcel today. I only wish my personal one would come, but I am very lucky and not grumbling. The weather after a long fine spell has again broken.

<u>22nd September 1942</u>
Tomorrow I shall have been commissioned three years. James Kilgorn came back from hospital and brought back the news of the death of Hoppy (Hopkinson, who is from this camp) and also De Pree (Seaforths) who was electrocuted in a tunnel at Dössel.[6] All the Grands Blessés[7] are now leaving this camp for Rotenburg IX-A/Z.[8] Dössel has now been finally broken up. Geoffrey McNab, who has passed the Board, is going and I am very sorry.

I have quite a collection of caterpillars these days: I have about six cocoons. General Fortune is very keen and I am looking after three of his as well. Any new varieties are sent along to me!

<u>25th September 1942</u>
The Grands Blessés, padres and doctors left yesterday for IX-A/Z. About thirty left in all and in their places forty-eight others have come from IX-A/Z, so that with the extra eighteen we are very full again. Have finished my embroidered map, which is now on loan to the library where it hangs. A new officer arrived in this camp last night who was in England ten days ago. It is three years ago since I last saw Joyce and Tony, one thousand and ninety-six days! German General inspected camp today.

<u>27th September 1942</u>
Swiss Commission arrived yesterday to make their usual inspection. The reprisals on our letters, also Stoker's case, were put to them to take up as best they can.

<u>29th September 1942</u>
The whole camp told to pack and prepare to leave at one hour's notice from tomorrow! A nice little bombshell to shake us out of our lethargy.

<u>30th September 1942</u>
Search of all kit. All our private kit taken. The whole camp then crowded into the dining hall for eight hours, not allowed out AT ALL. Latrine buckets

provided. Then we were read the 'Pasteur' allegations[9] and knew that we were in for another reprisal!

Needless to say, the reprisal applies to this camp and the Lower Camp only.[10] The following is a verbatim copy:

Declaration of the German Supreme Command,
concerning the measures taken at Oflag IX-A/H,
Spangenberg, September 30, 1942

It is only now that the German Supreme Command has got knowledge of the incidents which took place on board the troop ship 'Pasteur' taking German prisoners of war from Suez to South Africa. The German POW officers, among them two generals and one Knight of the Knighthood of the Iron Cross, were lodged in the forecastle of the D Deck while the other ranks were placed in the forecastle of the E Deck.

After a stay of one day in the port of Suez and a two days' voyage, the senior German officers and one medical officer were placed in solitary confinement in small arrest cells without any explanation. The next night, at midnight, the remaining officers were awakened by shouts and guards with drawn pistols forced them to a place of the stern of E Deck. The officers were not allowed to take anything along but a blanket and they had no time to dress. Like criminals, the officers had to pass a line of heavily armed guards, who insulted some of them and committed acts of violence.

It was only after a ten hour stay on the E Deck that the POWs were informed by the Officer Commanding Troops, Lt Col. Walsh, that he had ordered a thorough baggage examination and bodily search of the officers. Lt Col. Walsh tried to justify this measure remarking that he was of the opinion that the POWs had the intention to seize the ship.

The futile bodily search of the almost naked German officers, who had previously been deprived of all their personal belongings and who had already been searched several times before, took about two hours for itself. The search was not carried out under the supervision of British officers but by the rank and file alone. The examination of the baggage by South African and Belgian guards was dragged on for two days. Then the uniforms, linen and other belongings were heaped together in wild disorder by the guards and afterwards thrown into the officers mess room. The condition of the uniforms and other property clearly evidenced that the baggage had not only been searched but systematically looted. A large part of the uniforms and equipment was missing and the rest was partly torn, cut to pieces, soiled and robbed of all military badges of rank and distinction. In addition all pockets had been emptied, and almost all valuables stolen. Furthermore the dictionaries, educational and other books as well as games which the POWs had taken along were missing. Their suitcases and army cots, purchased with their own money under permission given by the former Camp Commandant, were not returned to them. All indispensable toilet articles as razors, combs, soap, etc. as well as all food and tobacco had disappeared without exception.

During the whole time used for the examination of the baggage and for the bodily search, the German officers received no food and therefore had to go hungry and thirsty for twenty-two hours. It was only after a stay of several days below deck in insufficiently ventilated rooms and in unbearable heat that the officers were permitted out in the open. The German orderlies were not allowed to attend to their officers. Upon arrival at Durban, officers had to leave the ship, clad only in underwear, bathing trunks or pyjamas and were exhibited to the mob of the port in this degrading costume, unwashed and unshaven. Most of the articles taken for examination were not returned.

To remedy the wrong done to the German POWs and in order to prevent similar offences, the German Supreme Command has informed the War Office in London of the following demands:

1) That the British Government officially expresses her regrets at the way the baggage was examined and the bodily search was conducted on board the SS 'Pasteur'. These regrets are to be expressed to all the officers concerned in the Canadian Camps, who, for this purpose, are to be assembled at roll call.

2) Full indemnity for the stolen private property of the POWs has to be made.

3) Declaration of the British Government concerning the measures taken to prevent similar occurrences.

4) Admission of Representatives of the Protecting Power to any departure and arrival of overseas transports.

Although up to now it has been the earnest endeavour of the German Supreme Command to treat the British POWs with chivalrous consideration, it is not possible to afford them more respect and inviolability of personal rights than are conceded to the German POWs in British hands. Therefore the German Supreme Command orders, taking effect from today, to give a small number of British POWs the same treatment as the German POWs had to suffer. It will however expressly abstain from repeating in all details the degradations inflicted on the German POW officers by the British authorities. Taking effect on 30 September 1942 the following measures have been ordered regarding the treatment of the British officers in Oflag IX-A Spangenberg.

1. ALL personal and common luggage including sanitary and cosmetic articles as soap, sponges, toothbrushes, towels, razors, etc. are to be taken away.

2. Knives, forks, scissors of every description are to be taken away.

3. All badges of rank, pips, crowns, if necessary shoulder straps and all ribbons, decorations, cockades and braids (if they can be easily and quickly removed without doing considerable damage to the uniform) are to be removed.

4. All officers are to be deprived of the service of their orderlies. These measures will be recalled immediately if and as soon as the British Government will have complied with the demands of the German Supreme Command. The British Government has been informed of the measures taken at Oflag IX-A Spangenberg by the Representatives of the Protecting Power.

1st October 1942

Today were returned to us our caps, coats and uniforms with all badges, medal ribbons of rank, etc. torn off. Everything else has been taken. We are allowed no soap or razors or brushes or towels, no books, eating utensils, etc., etc. We are left with what we stand up in!

3rd October 1942

Had a parcel from Egypt. Everyone in good cheer. No reprisals on our food luckily. We have been issued with one spoon each from the kitchen and one plate.

Theodore E. Casdagli, 1871 – 1942.

Oflag IX-A/H, the moat. 6 September 1942. © ICRC

5th October 1942

The moat was put out of bounds today owing to notices put up by us. The Germans have brought special guards with machine guns posted all round the battlements! Peter Dollar put up a notice 'Terror Angriffe in Progress'[11] whereupon the Germans closed the moat. Consequently, I put up a notice 'SS Pasteur – Promenade Deck Closed'.

8th October 1942

A Rolex watch, which I ordered from Switzerland months ago and never expected to see, arrived today – it is a beauty and has my name engraved on it.[12]

9th October 1942

There was a search of rooms today to see if we had concealed any soap, combs, knives, etc. The Germans have decided to degrade us to the fullest extent of their powers.

We heard today of the chaining of all the prisoners caught at Dieppe.[13] Reprisals are the fashion these days. I now have ten days' beard, like everyone else, including General Fortune.

11th October 1942

We hear on the German wireless that we have now chained German prisoners of war in England.[14]

12th October 1942

Usual parole walk but we were not allowed through the village. No doubt the Germans do not wish to exhibit the state they have reduced us to, that is, OUTWARDLY because our spirits are very high and everyone is getting very proud of his beard! The letter ban has now been lifted but may be re-imposed in November! Water is very short, owing to the drought.

15th October 1942

The armed Guard, here since 30th September, have returned to Kassel whence they came. Apparently serious trouble was expected.

16th October 1942

No water in the camp or village. Situation acute. However, we continue very cheerful. We could not wash even if there was water, so what the hell!

17th October 1942

Water situation still bad. Latrines have been dug in the moat.

COMITÉ INTERNATIONAL DE LA CROIX-ROUGE

AGENCE CENTRALE DES PRISONNIERS DE GUERRE

Rappeler dans la réponse :

SBrit
AM/mns   RBO 9/4061   GENÈVE,   Oct.13th.
                        Palais du Consell-Général   1942

Chèques postaux I. 5527
Téléphone 4 23 05
Télég. "INTERCROIXROUGE"

Geprüft
2
Oflag IX A

Lt. Col. E. MILLER,
Senior British Officer,
OFLAG IX A/H

Dear Sir,

        We shall feel much obliged if you will
kindly perform the painful duty of advising
Major Alexis CASDAGLI, POW No.3311, that we
have received the following message from Cairo –

" PRIERE PREVENIR MAJOR ALEXIS CASDAGLI 3311
  CAMP 9 AH ALLEMAGNE DESOLEE AVISER DECES
  PERE CATHERINE CASDAGLI REPONSE PAYEE"

        We should also thank you to kindly
convey to Major Casdagli our deepest sympathy
in his great loss.

        Thanking you in advance for your kind
assistance in this matter, we remain,

Rec:- Oct 20th 1942.
Replied.

                        Yours faithfully,
                        Comité International de la Croix-Rouge
                    p.o. Agence centrale des prisonniers de guerre
                        GENÈVE

Letter from CIRC, 13 October 1942.

Acc.réc.av.tél.exp.9.11.42 mns

Dear Sir,   I thank you very much for your letter
of Oct 13" No.S.Brit Ar/mns REO 9/4061 concerning
Major Cardaqli, the contents of which he has been
informed.

He would be very grateful if you would send the
following cable

E Cardaqli and Sons Cairo Egypt.
I deepest sympathy. am well. Dont worry I recvd.
He has asked me to express to you his very sincere
thanks for your kindness and sympathy.

Yours faithfully.

B.T. Murray Major
for. S.B.O. Upper Camp

PS Col Miller asked me to get this off quickly
and is away temporarily which prevents
him from signing personally

6 NOV. 1942   Com. Cairo DI 1548

RBO 9/4061

Letter from Maj. G. Murray, 22 October 1942.

20th October 1942
Letter arrived for me from Geneva today telling me of Father's death. They sent me also a reply-paid cable to Cairo. I can hardly believe I shall never see the old man again. More letters in today, also a parcel from Turkey.

23rd October 1942
Repatriation Commission[15] arrived today and five officers passed the Board. They were shocked at our conditions and the general state of the camp, as I should also have said that all the orderlies have been removed. One of the few books in the camp is my New Testament, which I had in my pocket and it escaped the search. It is a great joy to me. I have a lovely beard.

24th October 1942
A German general inspected the kitchen today! I hope he was satisfied?

27th October 1942
All our kit which is stored in town is to be searched – no doubt with the usual German thoroughness! Still no signs of an end to it all. Our teeth have certainly suffered and the lack of a toothbrush or ANY means of cleaning our teeth is a very serious matter.

30th October 1942
Letters coming in now. Joyce has had a letter from General Kaffatos. He said he would write.

4th November 1942
A parcel arrived for me today from the German Red Cross! It had presumably been sent from the Hamsons[16] to the Turkish Embassy in Berlin. Chiefly sardines and gym shoes.

7th November 1942
We discovered today in the moat a rotten old tree stump that has been attacked by some fungus, which has rendered it completely phosphorescent![17] We have it in our room and it is an astonishing sight and gives off quite a lot of light.

11th November 1942
Armistice Day service today and the usual two minutes silence.[18]

19th November 1942
Sent five Xmas cards today. Our beards are terrific now! I have a beautiful

black beard in contrast to General Fortune who has a beautiful white one!

26th November 1942
Swiss Legation came today; they had not heard of our conditions in spite of the repeated letters sent by General Fortune. We now know that the Germans held up those letters!! The only news the Legation had was from the Repatriation Committee[19] who reported to them our plight. They were very disgusted at our treatment and our appearance must be seen to be believed!![20]

27th November 1942
International YMCA arrived today. Still no news of reprisal ending.

28th November 1942
Order read out on parade today by German Commandant that the reprisal was at an end. It was met in dignified silence, I expect he expected cheers. Sixty days without soap, shaving or a toothbrush will not be quickly forgotten. Anyway, we stuck it out alright. We are particularly gratified that according to the order the German Government got NO satisfaction from the British Government. The reprisal was removed as the Germans considered that we, the officers of this Oflag, had been 'sufficiently punished' – what had we done anyway!! Our kit was returned to us from the village store today.

Room 13.

Names and regimental colours of the POWs are on their bunk beds. Their initials mark their place at the table. The initials in the top wall are of two escapees. The wireless is under the floorboards, right of the menu. A bit of coal is next to the stove. The Years Panel was enlarged to add '1944' and '1945'. The embroidery was hung on the wall with a piece of cardboard covering the Union Jack as displaying national flags was not allowed. On it, 'Do Not Pull Down' was written in German. Most Germans coming into Room 13 pulled the flap down and said 'This is forbidden!' whereupon Casdagli would reply 'You're displaying the Union Jack, not me!' 430 x 460 mm

10. CHARMING PEOPLE

2nd December 1942
Medical inspection of all officers by the Germans. I am told I am on the list to go to hospital to be operated on for my rupture. I still wear my truss and do not think I am any worse; still, an operation is the thing, if it can be done. Weather very cold. We are only getting one quarter of last year's coal issue!

4th December 1942
Red Cross have written that owing to transport difficulties we are to get one parcel every fourteen days instead of one a week; added to the fact that private food parcels from Egypt, America, etc., have also stopped, we shall be hungry again.

10th December 1942
Hot showers are now cut down to one every fourteen days. Weather much colder. Got some new wood shavings for my bed which had got very, very hard indeed.

15th December 1942
Swiss Commission arrived today to check up on the removal of the reprisal. Our letters posted to them on 1st October only reached them in Berlin at the end of November as the Germans had held them up! They say their news of the Pasteur affair took from March to September to get through! Aren't the Germans charming? Weather milder again. We have been sending from here clothes, books and tobacco to the Channel Island deportees,[1] also the Dieppe prisoners of war. In all we have sent 600 books, 30,000 cigarettes and 50 lb tobacco. Not bad for a camp of less than two hundred.

24th December 1942
Carol Service in the library. Xmas has come round again. I read the lesson last Sunday from St John. I have made a bookmark which our room are giving to General Fortune at Xmas. Very cold again.

25th December 1942
Splendid day. Church in the morning. Helped serve the orderlies lunch. We had our big meal in the evening in Room 13. Our Red Cross Xmas parcel was the foundation of it but we had other stuff saved up. Orderlies' party in the

evening, had some homebrewed 'hooch'.[2] There was a little drunkenness but nothing compared to last year. I only hope General Kaffatos had as good an Xmas as we did. Actually we had food from England, USA, South America, Turkey, Egypt and Portugal! That shows how kind people have been to us. We are very optimistic.[3] Since 6th December I have been working on an embroidered plan of our room from a scale drawing by Bertie MacLeay. Much colder again.

30th December 1942
Heavy snow and frost. Much colder. The coal ration is so small that we feel very cold in our room these days.

1st January 1943
Had a great party last night: very cheery. I must have shaken hands with about two hundred people. Took part in a small sketch – appropriately as the radio announcer![4] Letters very bad these days and none from Joyce since 5th November.

3rd January 1943
The German camp doctor, Oberst Brangs, has now been moved from here and there is little chance of getting my hernia operated on. They say he was 'too friendly' with us!

6th January 1943
Have started making a skating and curling rink in the moat.[5] I am in charge of skating. We can only get very little water to flood it and it will be a long job. John Russell (Squadron Leader, DFC) leaves for an RAF camp tomorrow. Really cold now.

10th January 1943
We have actually started skating, twenty-two degrees frost F. We have twelve pairs of skates; I find I can skate quite well still. The rink is thirty by forty yards but rather bumpy.

12th January 1943
Another search today but nothing of mine taken. Received today the obituary notices of Father's death sent me by Mum through Switzerland. Here is the final paragraph from a long appreciation in the 'Manchester Guardian': 'Perhaps our greatest appreciation would be for us to take an example from his life, moulding ourselves to go through life with that same determination

for honest and straightforward dealing, unhesitating frankness for all that is just and right, at the same time maintaining the desire not to associate with unpleasantness.'

13th January 1943
Thaw set in, skating off. We have been allowed an extra issue of coal for our room, as we are ten in it. We can do with it too.

16th January 1943
We have been here a year now – in a way it has passed quickly.

21st January 1943
An Education Committee visited the camp today. Still thawing. Letters few and far between, also parcels. We are back on a Red Cross parcel a week, which is great news. It is the personal and private parcels which are bad.

31st January 1943
Not much political or war news will be found in this journal – for obvious reasons. We are, however, very, very cheerful.[6] Quite like spring weather. Not a match in the camp now.[7] The canteen can hardly produce anything – not surprising. The Swiss have provided us with some toilet paper, the first for many months. I have found that the 'Völkischer Beobachter' is much harder than the 'Frankfurter Zeitung'[8] which is about the best of the German newspapers.[9] The YMCA have also produced some pencils. Had a Red Cross message from the Naxakis[10] in Crete. Nice of them to remember me.

3rd February 1943
Private parcels have now nearly stopped and Egypt, Switzerland, USA and Portugal are no longer allowed to send. It makes a considerable difference to our comfort but we shall manage alright.

10th February 1943
Monthly medical examination by German doctor, which is an absolute farce. Colonel Wilson, RAMC, has come here from Ober-Malsfeld Hospital, about thirteen miles north. He has been kicked out by the Germans after doing magnificent work for British prisoners of war for two and a half years. Am doing a lot of reading and have devoured all the Arctic and Antarctic books in the library. Reading of other people's hardships helps one to realise that one's own are negligible in comparison; we have no reason for self-pity here – at least not now.

Taken by the CIRC, 23 March 1943.

Horlicks Tablets

German matchbox labels.

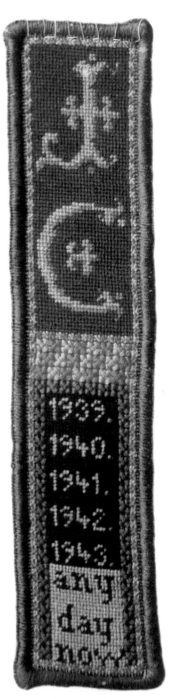

Any Day Now.
50 x 320 mm

19th February 1943

Surprise search last night and early this morning. Have just completed a haversack made out of Turkish parcel wrappings. Sent home a piece of embroidery to Joyce via Portugal. Weather mild. The Guard Company have changed.

26th February 1943

Still mild. Have now had two splendid parcels from the Rotary Club of Chicago.[11] Letters are still very bad from England. We have enough food these days.

2nd March 1943

Big raid last night. Received a clothing parcel from Joyce today. Germans confiscated my beautiful corduroy trousers – very annoying – otherwise magnificent parcel. We have sent 16,600 cigarettes and 15½ lb of tobacco to Ober-Malsfeld Hospital.

4th March 1943

Sent home another piece of embroidery and a bookmark. Have nearly finished a table centre and will then start an evening bag each for Joyce and Judy.[12] Weather very mild. Jack Poole[13] (60th Rifles, DSO, OBE, MC) gave me a fine blanket.

8th March 1943

McDermott has arrived from Gabey so we have had some fresh news. Have started Joyce's bag. Operations for hernia are definitely OFF, say the Germans.

12th March 1943

RC left today for Rotenburg; we do not yet know who will come in their place.

16th March 1943

Some officers have come from the Straffe-Lager at IV-C[14] and have brought us a little news. They were all at Laufen[15] and mostly are RE. Sherman, an Australian doctor who was with the Seventh General Hospital in Crete, has moved to Ober-Malsfeld to take Wilson's place as Wilson has gone to Lamsdorf Stalag.[16] Sherman came to tea in our room and told us some amazing stories. Six thousand Russians died in a year at the Stalag he came from. He was their Medical Officer so this is first-hand and no rumour. He told us incredible stories of the rations they were given: how they used to eat grass collected in their compounds and boiled on the incinerator.[17]

McLeod (Cameronian, Commander) has come in from Tunis with the latest news – most interesting.[18] Weather still very fine and am working regularly on the cricket 'pitch' for the coming season.

18th March 1943
Medical inspection farce today. Weather colder. Lack of notebooks and paper will probably mean rather shorter entries in this journal than heretofore. We had a sports meeting on 13th March. I acted as timekeeper. I would certainly have taken part had I been fit. My swelling is not much bigger and does not trouble me much.

25th March 1943
McGavin, a parachute doctor from Tunis, is here. We seem to collect all the odds and sods in this camp! Much work to do on the cricket pitch. On 23rd, International Red Cross came to the camp and asked to see me. They took my photograph to send to Joyce and to Mum and also brought me a message from Mum in Cairo,[19] which was very nice of them.

27th March 1943
Two officers, Corran Purdon and Dick Morgan (St Nazaire Commandos) got away last night and are still at large – a beautiful break. Good luck to them. Germans in the hell of a flap as can be imagined. Tomorrow is the anniversary of the St Nazaire Raid.

28th March 1943
Invited to the St Nazaire party which was a very good show. One hundred and thirty Americans are now at Rotenburg – have sent them my Red Cross blanket and a shirt in the collection we have made here: they are very short of kit. Had a letter from Michael Parish (Notts. Yeom.)! He had not forgotten the bully I gave him in Crete – he says it was a good investment – it certainly proved to be. He came to my tent the night before he escaped and I was able to give him the few things he wanted, and he promised if ever he got back to Cairo he would go and see Mother and he has.[20]

2nd April 1943
Corran and Dick have been caught again. They were brought back this evening and given a great cheer. Bad weather and lost food let them down. My box of Horlicks[21] has played its part. Lecture this evening by the parachute doctor.

3rd April 1943
Attempted escape tonight by Black Campbell and Yule from IV-C. Very courageous effort from the moat, it just did not come off.[22] Another big flap by the Germans. Shots fired but luckily no one hurt.

5th April 1943
An American RC padre has arrived here, Kane by name.[23] The first American we have yet seen. He comes from Iowa. Bad weather these days.

6th April 1943
Swiss Legation arrived today on their usual quarterly visit. Nothing startling.

7th April 1943
Swedish YMCA came today: no news.

10th April 1943
My birthday, the second inside. Life drags on and the wasted days pass.

16th April 1943
Several more officers in and several more orderlies gone. The old, old story of overcrowding and lack of orderlies. Even the schoolroom is now a dormitory. Received an excellent photograph of Tony – how I long to see him again!

17th April 1943
Have started running round the moat before breakfast. Ram (F. S. Ramsay, Worcesters) and I do a mile (eight laps) at 7.30 am. We do it regularly and feel all the better for it. It is satisfying to know one can still take fairly strenuous exercise and improve at it, as we undoubtedly are doing with practice.

22nd April 1943
Big search today, in which the Germans had a fair measure of success. Weather very bad – wet. The long weeks drag past.

Oflag IX-A/H, the cricket pitch. © ICRC

The moustache.

Oflag IX-A/H. 'Sunbathing area'
in German, English and French.
© ICRC

11. REST IN PEACE

<u>29th April 1943</u>
Nark-baiting[1] has officially started – and stopped! The nark is Herr Detmering,[2] a horrible bit of work. He has seen the General and promised to mend his ways.

On Monday there was a treasure hunt for which I did not enter – but had a little amusement by putting out false clues, most of them rather rude! It ended by my having to apologise to Lt Colonel Gamble, the organiser.

<u>1st May 1943</u>
The German authorities have requested General Fortune to go to Katyn[3] to inspect the alleged mass graves of Polish officers. Naturally, he has refused to go unless he is authorised by the British Government. Our hosts are very strange people!

<u>2nd May 1943</u>
Our floor was searched again today for the nth time! The Germans are very 'windy' just now. They are putting more wire up everywhere and generally being very active. Cricket started today. We have put in a lot of work on the ground, which is in good condition. After all, it is only a mud patch – but we get an incredible amount of fun.

<u>14th May 1943</u>
Fine sunny weather. Have shaved off my beautiful moustache today in celebration of the final clearance of the enemy from North Africa.[4] We have now an invasion 'sweep' on the date of landing in Europe. My day is Tony's birthday, June 12th. We are having splendid fine weather just now.

<u>21st May 1943</u>
We heard the bombing of the German dams reported in the papers and the wildest rumours are going round about flooding, damage and casualties.[5] I have now stepped up my running in the morning to sixteen laps (two and a quarter miles) daily and I keep a log of exact distance run.

<u>27th May 1943</u>
Am now reading all the books I can find on birds. Plenty of practical experience from the birds nesting in and around the moat.

<u>1st June 1943</u>
Guy German (Leicesters)[6] escaped today but not for long – no luck.

The American officers came to see the camp today, prior to starting an American Oflag. They came from Rotenburg. They were Lt Colonel Van Vliet (aged twenty-nine) and Major Sturgeon. The former made his famous remark on hearing latrine paper was not available and issued now by the Germans only to invalids and pregnant women.[7]

Lt Colonel Van Vliet, another American and a South African Colonel had been sent to Katyn.[8] They went under written protest and did not give their parole. They absolutely refuse to discuss what they saw, so that, from a propaganda point of view, the Germans have not gained very much![9]

<u>2nd June 1943</u>
Repatriation Commission arrived today but only Tracker Richardson passed the Board. Rumours that the Grands Blessés are going to the Lower Camp and that the Lower Camp moves to Rotenburg.

Still reading bird books.

<u>3rd June 1943</u>
Sent another bit of embroidery to Joyce.

Inoculated yesterday TAB and was very ill after it – my own fault for not cancelling my run. Spent most of the day on my bed. I was better by the evening.

<u>13th June 1943</u>
Gordon-Duff (Eton – Rifle Brigade, brother-in-law to Rodney Palmer) has arrived here after four months in a German gaol. Nice chap; good cricketer obviously.

<u>14th June 1943</u>
Yesterday there was a very big search in which our tunnel was found during the night.[10] Pity – still it had a good run. Our room, No. 13, was also very carefully and severely searched, floorboards ripped up, etc. – queer people these Germans – still, it's their floor!

<u>16th June 1943</u>
Great activity by the Germans. Generals come and inspect the tunnel. The room where the spoil had been put was also found. In fact, a clean sweep.

My February clothing parcel arrived and as usual it was just perfect. Have started Judy's bag.

18th June 1943
Yesterday fifteen officers left for IV-C, in fact all the ones who came from there a few months ago plus Tom Stallard, Corran Purdon and Dick Morgan. We never saw Guy German again and expect he is there too.[11] We presume they are looked on as being guilty for the tunnel! We have been very busy clearing away all the spoil from the room it was in – the orderlies were ordered to do it but it was quite obviously OUR work, which everyone is doing willingly, although a little sadly at the wasted effort! We had finished the job at 2.30 pm – starting in shifts from 9.00 am.

19th June 1943
This morning our room was again searched and more floorboards taken up. This time the wireless set, which was under the boards by the window, was found! No use moaning, we had a really good run. Amazing we kept it as long as we did! We now await repercussions! This month has certainly been an unfortunate one for the camp, but we keep cheerful in the knowledge that we are WINNING the war!

25th June 1943
Another general arrived yesterday – visited the tunnel and our room. They seem almost as proud of the tunnel and its workmanship as we are!

27th June 1943
I had the most vivid dream last night that Theo[12] had been killed in an accident, then heard today of the tragic death at Rotenburg of Brigadier Claude Nicholson last night by falling from his window. Brigadier Claude Nicholson was in command at Calais, 1940.[13]

29th June 1943
The Germans tried their propaganda on us today, sticking up placards with photographs of Katyn all over the camp and also leaving literature in our rooms while we were on parade – they did not remain there for long as can be imagined. The Germans have forbidden General Fortune to attend Brigadier Nicholson's funeral.

3rd July 1943
Yesterday the goldfinches nesting on the inner battlement saw their brood safely fly away: the first at 8.00 am, the last and fifth at 1.40 p.m. They all cleared the moat easily – very exciting. Our counter-propaganda has stopped by mutual agreement with the Germans that they stop theirs. Our victory!!

Swallowtail 1943. 175 x 110 mm

12. FOUR YEARS OF WAR

<u>8th July 1943</u>
Further searches by the Germans have discovered a certain amount of stuff including 'the hole in the wall'.[1] Read the lesson last Sunday evening. Three Grands Blessés, all amputations, have arrived here.

<u>16th July 1943</u>
Bill Mercer (RA) arrived from Ober-Malsfeld yesterday having been out fourteen days; Bill Edwards who was with him is still out. The Germans are still trying their propaganda on us! After all this time! However long we stay here, they will NEVER understand us! Nor we them – of that I am quite certain.

<u>23rd July 1943</u>
The goldfinches have built again in the same nest and she is already sitting. Gave a talk in the evening on 'Squash Rackets'[2] with J. F. M. Lightly (Tower Hamlets).

Bill Edwards has now been brought back. He got to within five miles of freedom and saw the mountains of Switzerland! We are having glorious weather.

<u>28th July 1943</u>
The biggest thrill we have ever had! Forty-eight Flying Fortresses[3] in perfect formation flew over the camp on their way to bomb Kassel, which we heard clearly. It is quite impossible to describe our feelings – how we cheered! May this be the beginning!

<u>29th July 1943</u>
We are suffering now from an acute water shortage. No showers and no water in the camp from nine to one and one to four and only a trickle after that. Most unpleasant. We have had roasting hot weather since 13th July.

Mussolini's 'retirement' has put us in great heart.[4]

Still continue regular running before breakfast.

<u>30th July 1943</u>
What a TERRIFIC day! One hundred and forty-two Flying Fortresses came right over the camp in waves in glorious sunshine on their way to Kassel again. I saw two German fighters, heard the cannon fire and saw one of our planes hit. Eight parachutes came out as far as we could see but the

plane did not actually crash. One of the parachutes landed literally within a mile of the camp. The eight of them, all Americans, were brought to our Kommandantur.[5] The chap we saw made a dive for the woods but was caught.

5th August 1943
Visit of Protecting Power. Interviewed them about mail to and from Egypt. Morgan was sent to Rotenburg at a moment's notice. We are now one hundred and eighty here.

6th August 1943
Morgan returned today making our number one hundred and eighty-one, or one more than capacity according to the Germans. Presumably, his move was to fool the Swiss – amazing people, Germans!

12th August 1943
We have had an amazing spell of hot weather, almost a month with the heat from eighty-six degrees to eighty-eight in the shade. It broke some days ago.

The water situation is again acute! We have never been in a camp yet where water and light were in any degree adequate. Bad light for reading and little water for washing have been the order for the day. The latrines now are smelling to high heaven and have to be flushed by hand with the water we have saved from our morning wash and shave. No prospects of enough water for some time. Baths (our fortnightly one!) have been cancelled.

The village is full of evacuees from bombed towns and the consumption of water in the village must be many times above normal.

This year our Rooms 13–15 have beaten all the others at cricket and last year Rooms 9–12, in which I then was, were also champions. I captained Lancs. and Yorks. the other day and we only lost by seven runs. Very exciting finish.

19th August 1943
We are all in good heart and anxiously awaiting the next military developments. Plenty of air activity these days.

My May parcel arrived yesterday. I have been lucky lately. German general arrived today to inspect.

27th August 1943
Read through Maurice Wilson's 'Pharaohs' Emeralds' to correct Egyptian names, etc., and put him right about Cairo geography. It is pretty average tripe but may sell as a thriller.

Water is still a big problem, no pulling of chains yet. It is one MONTH since we last had a shower! Major Golding, RADC, is here temporarily and I have an appointment with him tomorrow.

3rd September 1943
Four years of war today. Have had two appointments with the dentist and one more sees me finished. The ravages of the last few years are being efficiently checked. Colossal luck for me that Golding should come.

Wrote a business letter to Joyce and sent a Power of Attorney to Frank Hargrove.[6]

10th September 1943
The water situation after getting a little better is worse again. I wonder if prisoners in England undergo what we do here in the way of lighting, overcrowding and ordinary elementary sanitation? Flap at 9.30 p.m. last night. Attempted escape. All my teeth have now been attended to.

11th September 1943
The exit of Italy from the war has put us in great heart and we feel even more optimistic.[7] We had a tremendous feed to celebrate!

19th September 1943
The weather is better but the three chief miseries for a prisoner, other than hunger and thirst, are ever present: (a) overcrowding, (b) bad lighting, (c) sanitation troubles. Cricket still going on, and I continue my early morning runs.

That hardy annual 'repatriation' has cropped up again, but not a soul believes a word of it; those concerned who were fooled in 1940 take less account of it than anyone else.

24th September 1943
Life drags on – four years ago yesterday I entered the army! And four years tomorrow since I last saw Joyce and Tony. Water situation better. Weather colder, only thirty-four degrees F yesterday. Still run twenty laps (two and a half miles) every morning. I have now done 2,540 laps. My hernia only worries me a little and is no worse. Just as well.

25th September 1943
Five officers from Italy arrived today – terrific excitement to hear all their news and what their life had been like in Italy. New blood in the camp always makes a difference. Yesterday we had a talk by Python Pemberton on the 'rest camp'[8] in Berlin to which he had been sent. We are all even more convinced than ever that the German mentality is beyond our comprehension.

On this date there were British Officers in German Prison Camps who had been in MANACLES almost a year!

Q u e s t i o n n a i r e
=======================================

You are requested to express frankly your suggestions of how to improve Life in Camp. Any honest cooperation will not only be highly appreciated but seems to be necessary. Anything will be done to bring into effect any reasonable wish.

Please write your answer on blank of this paper and hand your suggestions back to us either signed or anonymously, since we want to learn your unbiased opinion.

Spangenberg, the 12th of October 1943
Oflag IX A/H

Questionnaire, 12 October 1943.

Fuck Hitler bookmark.
With Morse code, POW number and colours of Harrow School.
250 x 55 mm

30th September 1943
Anniversary of the 'Pasteur' reprisals, which none of us is ever likely to forget. For indignity and conditions of squalor, it can hardly be exceeded.

5th October 1943
Six Allied airmen from one of the bombers which crashed near here were buried today in the village.

There was a terrific night raid on Kassel on 3rd September and we had a splendid view of the fireworks from our window.

The Germans have today discovered that Robin Snook (RA) and Dick Lorraine (RE) are 'missing'.[9]

8th October 1943
We have been strafed[10] nearly all week.

For three mornings including today we have spent from 10.00 am till 2.00 pm in the moat, while the building is searched. Cold and uncomfortable but well worth it to see the Germans well and truly rattled.

15th October 1943
Robin and Dick still 'missing'.

The Grands Blessés are really now on their way to England. After a false start, they all came back here again but they were used to that. Anyway, NOW they have made it. The Repatriation Board came to pass more people and Crash Keyworth (Bays) and Mercer (RA) passed.

Weather continues fine and cold, thirty-two point six degrees at 8.00 am.

No coal yet. A nuthatch is now a regular visitor for crumbs and margarine at our window. Have started to teach myself Spanish and intend to work hard.

22nd October 1943
Dick and Robin have been re-caught – they say near Darmstadt.[11] They are not likely to return here.

Water difficulties are again at their worst, and the long days accentuate the very bad lighting. I refused to send a reply to a 'Questionnaire' from the Germans as to how to improve our camp life! Can you beat it – when they still have British officers in German prison camps in manacles for the Dieppe show! The Swedish YMCA have confirmed they are still in chains after almost a year.

We hear that the Grands Blessés have arrived in Sweden.

Terrific raid on Kassel last night. Even bigger it seemed than 3rd October. It lasted one and a half hours and was thrilling and rather terrifying to watch.

24th October 1943
Still do my twenty laps every morning and it keeps me fit. Letters very bad just now. Weather much colder. They made us a small coal issue. Am making good progress at Spanish.

29th October 1943
Have been busy on the cricket ground. Have put a new surface to it. Hernia continues the same, no worse, which is just as well.

5th November 1943
Four degrees frost F this morning at 8.00 am. Walks on parole are now stopped owing to the feeling of the villagers. Over two thousand refugees in addition have just arrived from Kassel since the last raid. Water position worse than usual and there are threats of latrines in the moat, etc. The enormous increase of population in the village affects us particularly as the village is going to tap the reservoir that feeds the Castle, which is hopelessly inadequate in any case. This place used to be a Forestry School with sixty students!

Still continue my morning runs. Jack Poole is leaving for VII-B.[12] He had applied to go a long time ago. Rumours of two British generals coming here.

12th November 1943
Armistice Day service yesterday as usual. Weather cold and wet. Lighting shocking, water still precarious. Two South African brigadiers arrived here last Sunday – they were caught in Italy on 21st October.[13]

Still working hard at Spanish.

18th November 1943
Colonel Tod (Scots Fusiliers), our SBO,[14] the best we are ever likely to have, was removed today to the Straffe-Lager at IV-C – with no reason being given by the Germans.

19th November 1943
Big air raid last night. Lights out from 8.00 pm till 11.00 pm. During the blackout, the guards fired at our 'fat lamps' in which we burn German margarine. Apparently the light must have been shining through, but even with electric lights on they have never fired in nearly two years. No warning given either. Rooms 17 and 8 had bullets right through the blackout windows and embedded in the far wall. There was also one through the dining hall window where there was a lecture on. No reason why several officers should not have been killed – it was not the Germans' fault! Nice people. I was in the

dining hall at the time and sitting just in line with the window; they did not shoot through – lucky for me.

26th November 1943

Air raids almost every night now. Went to the Kommandantur to meet the skating officer from the Bottom Camp. We are now able to send home our marks. I have sent back to Joyce one hundred and sixty pounds sterling.[15] Spanish progressing very well.

3rd December 1943

Big search today – army and civilians. Three-hour air raid; blackout last night. Weather cold, snow. Letters from home very few and slow. Life drags on and quite a lot of people, including myself, give it another year – others a month!

10th December 1943

Two officers have now been sent here from Cos,[16] so we have had some of the latest news. Winter has set in with snow and ice. Am nearing four thousand laps of early morning running. Yesterday I got some books from America – Penguins. Mail very slow.

17th December 1943

Frost. Still doing my two and a half miles in spite of the weather. Spanish progresses. Have just completed six table mats with butterfly design. No mail lately. Not enough snow yet to make a skating rink. Yesterday we were allowed to meet the Lower Camp at the sports ground and I saw and spoke to Ian Fernie, Harvey Wolstenholme and Ronnie Kay. There was a football match between the camps.

24th December 1943

Had letters today from Mum and Menda. Brigadier Tilney has now arrived here from Leros.[17] He had twenty-five days solitary before being sent here. Wet and damp. Saw dress rehearsal of Rupert Christie's pantomime – excellent show. Words and music all locally written by him, Colonel Newman (Essex) and Colonel Fraser (15/19 Hussars). Plenty of air activity these nights; lights out for hours on end. Not feeling much like a 'Merry' Xmas. Still doing my daily run and am pretty fit. The time drags by, but Spanish helps. Also am embroidering a cover to my New Testament in petit point.

31st December 1943

Finished my cover today. Snow falling. Ran this morning after being held

New Testament Cover.
175 x 110 mm

up five days by mud. I am held up surprisingly little by bad weather. Letters from Menda have upset me very much: have again tried to get permission to send her food and money.[18] General Fortune has written a special letter to the YMCA for me to try and get their people there to get in touch with her. Was feeling so depressed that I gave away my Xmas cake and chocolate biscuits – somehow I could not face eating them this year. Considering the misery of the rest of Europe, we useless prisoners are excessively well off.

7th January 1944
Weather cold but thawing. The long days are slowly dragging past. I still work at Spanish every day till lunchtime and run before breakfast. All the embroidery I have sent to Joyce has got home, so I decided to send the butterfly mats.

14th January 1944
We shall have been here two years in two days! Still very bad mail conditions for me, others seem to be luckier. We have had an exceptionally mild winter so far, contrary to forecasts. We heard our planes over on 11th, but owing to cloud only saw a few. The Germans are in many ways much more reasonable these days!

21st January 1944
The Swiss arrived today and remained from about 3.00 pm till 9.00 pm examining our complaints, etc. The chief are: overcrowding, bad lighting, mail, exercise space, the shooting incident, etc. Day before yesterday the German General in charge of all POWs, named Roettich, visited the camp and was much displeased. No news yet about sending food and money to Menda. My rupture pains me occasionally but nothing worse than usual. Another German general is expected in a day or so!

28th January 1944
Filthy weather – rain and mud. Nine Spanish magazines have come to me from Switzerland, which are most welcome. Still no letter from Joyce this month. The war drags on – one day it will end, I suppose. I have embroidered a letter which I shall send home to Tony.

Herr Reinhardt, Foreign Office German official (Consul in Liverpool before the war),[19] visited the camp today and interviewed General Fortune. Actually, they went for a walk together! Snow today but otherwise astonishingly mild.

The light in our room is very bad indeed. I sit in the library whenever possible, where it is better. The censoring of our letters is now done here instead of at Rotenburg, which may help to speed things up. My request to

Oflag IX/AH.
Germany.
Dear Tony,
            I am so glad to hear that you are
doing so well at school. I hope you always will
continue to try your hardest at work and play.
It is 1581 days since I saw you last but it will
not be long now. Do you remember when I fell
down the well? Look after Mummy till I get
home again. God bless you Love from
                                        Daddy.

January 1944.

Letter to Tony. 310 x 210 mm

send food and money to Menda was again refused today.

We are now allowed a hot shower per week instead of every fourteen days – which has been the case for the last two years! We have been collecting wood and this has made it possible.

11th February 1944
Potato rations cut by fifty per cent since Monday! Letters coming through better. My embroidered letter to Tony left on 2nd February. Spanish and running continue regularly. Thick snow here last few days. Usual medical farce this morning. Am now as used to my truss as ever I shall be. It is quite a good one. I am heading for one thousand days in the bag – three years in June – what an age and what a waste of active life. Tant pis![20] It might be much worse, we are anyway WINNING.

18th February 1944
Weather much colder and we have had rough skating and curling since yesterday; it means a lot of work on the 'rink'. It has been a big job getting enough ice to form.[21] We are hoping the frost will continue. Still do my Spanish, at which I have improved a lot, and still run every day but have stopped my embroidery as I have no more cottons. My February parcel should arrive soon. Menda was well on 14th January but they are having a pretty rotten time. The war drags on.

An opportunity has arisen to change camps. A new camp has been formed by the Germans at Hadamar, Oflag XII-B, composed entirely of officers who have been brought to Germany from prisoner of war camps in Italy on the capitulation of that country. Volunteers from our camp have to be of the rank of major or above. There's been little response, most people quoting the saying 'better the devil you know than the devil you don't.'

25th February 1944
This week has been much enlivened by air activity. On 23rd saw two hundred and fifty of our bombers and about fifty fighters. Two 150-gallon petrol tanks, made by Lockheed Corporation, Burbank, California, were picked up and brought to the Kommandantur; I actually saw them being dropped – no one knew what they were.[22]

Frost continues and skating and curling in FULL SWING and the ice is pretty good; we have started a second curling rink! Some splendid Spanish books have arrived for me from Switzerland.

Spangenberg Castle. 310 x 210 mm

13. PER ANUM AD ASTRA[1]

<u>28th February 1944</u>

I am taking the opportunity to move. It is almost March 1944 and I still cannot see the war ending for at least another year; the 'invasion', although always uppermost in our minds, has not yet become a reality. I have been at Spangenberg Castle, Oflag IX-A/H for over two years[2] and I am heartily tired of the place and its one hundred and ninety occupants, although among them I count some of my sincerest friends.

There are four of us who are due to move to the new camp. I suppose we all have our different reasons. One of my companions, Sam Griffith of the Welsh Regiment, was caught in Crete on the same day as myself in 1941 and we have been together ever since, so that it seems natural that we should still remain together, although we both made up our minds to move individually. The other two were caught in France in 1940, 'Chutney' Deighton, a 6'6" gunner, and Bob Wilby of the Tyneside Scottish, in private life a Conservative Party agent and no less voluble in captivity. The four of us, therefore, are to make the journey together.

<u>1st March 1944</u>

We leave tomorrow. This afternoon, Neil Rattray, our New Zealand 'security' officer, asked me to come to his room. In his room I found Sam and Chutney already there. He explained the reason for wanting to speak to us. It is considered that as our new camp, Oflag XII-B, is composed entirely of officers from Italy, it is unlikely that they will be in possession of a full set of War Office maps of Germany. Oflag IX-A/H, being an old-established camp, is well supplied with maps and can easily spare a full set. I do not propose to divulge how these maps came into the camps but the ingenious methods could fill a book.[3]

Neil explained to us that he wanted us to take some twelve maps with us and that the only safe way was 'per anum'.[4] German searches are very thorough affairs these days in 1944 and it is not unusual to be stripped to the buff for examination while one's personal belongings are always minutely searched in the usual methodical German manner. Bob Wilby is not to be a 'carrier' as he suffers rather badly from piles[5] and, although willing enough, it was thought by Neil that three of us could carry all that he wanted to send.

I had heard of this method of carrying maps and other small objects for escaping purposes but I had no personal experience. The three of us thought that at least it would be amusing to try once as well as contributing, as we

DATE	LAPS	TOTAL	RUNS.	DATE	LAPS	TOTAL
FEB 17	20	5020	276			
" 18	20	5040	277.			
" 19	20	5060	278			
" 20	20	5080	279.			
" 21	15	5095	280			
" 22	25	5120	281.			
" 23	20	5140	282			
" 24	20	5160	283.			
" 25	20	5180	284			
" 26	20	5200	285.			
" 27	20	5220	286			
" 28	20	5240	287			
" 29	20	5260	288			
MAR 1.						

Last page of early morning runs. 5,260 laps of 250 yards per lap completed over 288 mornings, totalling 1,315,000 yards or 747.16 miles.

128

hoped, to the escaping facilities in our new camp.

We are due to leave at 2.00 am in the morning and therefore the operation of 'inserting' the maps had to be carried out tonight as late as possible but in time to allow us to get back to our rooms from the hospital before the final night-count by the Germans.

Our appointment with Dr Jimmy James was at 9.45 pm and accordingly we all met in the hospital. On the table were three sinister-looking objects the thickness of a cigar and a little shorter than a half-corona, done up in rubber finger stalls. explained to us that the 'insertion' would be neither difficult nor painful but that, on arrival, we were to report at once to our new camp doctor to have the objects withdrawn. His words were true enough and, apart from a slight feeling of tight discomfort, we are none of us any the worse.

The only apprehension I have is if I can 'hold it' till tomorrow afternoon, when we are expected to reach our new camp at Hadamar – a matter of seventeen hours.

2nd March 1944

After practically no sleep, we were ready to leave at 2.00 am. I had decided to eat as little as possible but it was a freezing cold morning and I could not refuse the plate of hot porridge which our thoughtful cookhouse had provided for us and some tea before leaving at 2.30 am. Five of us left IX-A/H (Willy, Johnson, Deighton, Griffith and I), all majors. Still heavy snow and frost.

We caught the 4.30 am train from Spangenberg. Our average age is in the region of forty and we believed that the Huns no doubt would think that there would not be much likelihood of a break by any of us old gentlemen on the way. For my part, being doubly ruptured and wearing this abomination of a German-made truss, any idea of escaping did not enter my mind. But as it so turned out, we were so heavily guarded that it would have been virtually impossible even for the youngest and fittest escapee.

At Malsfeld three South Africans joined us, Lt Colonel Sherwell and Majors Patterson and Darlow, who had come from Rotenburg. Colonel Sherwell is a brother of G. R. and T. Y.[6] and knew Uncle X[7] very well and often played tennis with him.

We changed again at Treysa and then Giessen,[8] where we had a two hour wait. We were very well treated and taken to the civilian restaurant on the station. It was most refreshing to be in the outside world again and among civilians, women and children, instead of only men in uniform.

At 11.00 am the air raid alarm went and we had to go to a shelter with literally hundreds of women and children. It was an awkward time but their behaviour was exemplary. Our planes were droning overhead and there was

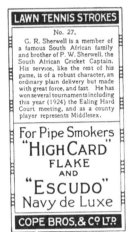

LAWN TENNIS STROKES

No. 27.

G. R. Sherwell is a member of a famous South African family and brother of P. W. Sherwell, the South African Cricket Captain. His service, like the rest of his game, is of a robust character, an ordinary plain delivery but made with great force, and fast. He has won several tournaments including this year (1924) the Ealing Hard Court meeting, and as a county player represents Middlesex.

For Pipe Smokers
"HIGH CARD"
FLAKE
AND
"ESCUDO"
Navy de Luxe

COPE BROS. & Cº Lᵀᴰ

G. R. SHERWELL
SERVICE STROKE

COPE BROS. & Cº Lᵀᴰ

A cigarette card of G.R. Sherwell.

T.Y. Sherwell.

Xenophon Casdagli.

no resentment shown to us and no fear or panic among them, which there might well have been. Later on, with the alarm still on and our planes still visible, we entrained for Limburg.

Then came our big thrill! A few minutes after leaving Giessen, one of our planes bombed the train – luckily with nothing very heavy! We saw one stick of incendiaries burst not more than thirty yards from the track and one of the guards reckoned a second-class carriage behind us was hit. It was pretty accurate bombing as the planes were very high. I now have the honour to have been bombed by four air forces, British, American, German and Italian!

At Limburg we again went to the restaurant for coffee, etc. – they made it for us from our own stuff. We then entrained for Hadamar after, for all of us, the most exciting and thrilling day in the last three years. We felt quite civilised again and more than a little shy and awkward at being in the big wide world again, instead of behind barbed wire.

OFLAG XII-B, HADAMAR

Oflag XII-B, general view and sports area. © ICRC

Oflag XII-B. Roll call. © ICRC

14. A PHOBIA OF BARBED WIRE

2nd March 1944

Since the last entry I have arrived at Hadamar, Oflag XII-B.[1] Suffice it to say, we arrived without further incident and not much the worse for wear at 5.00 pm and were ushered into the German Camp Office for documenting and searching. Ironically enough, the search was a very lenient one and, although our personal belongings were thoroughly examined and pulled about, we were not asked to strip. After the search we were passed into the camp, a converted boys' school.

We reported our arrival to the British adjutant and with one breath we asked to see the MO at once! This surprise request obviously caused some comment because we did not immediately disclose the reason for our urgent desire to see him without further delay. At length, we found the MI Room with Dr John Theron, South African Army, in charge. We explained to him our plight, which rather staggered him but he promised he would do what he could at once.

Sam Griffith was the first to be dealt with and he passed into an inner room with Doc Theron. Chutney and I waited patiently for about ten minutes when at last the door opened and out came Sam looking rather pale.

'Is it alright, Sam, did he get it out?' I asked anxiously.

'No,' he answered, 'he can't find it!'

Now, for the first time, I became a little apprehensive about the whole business. Sam continued,

'He bent me over a table and poked about with some forceps and every now and again gave an awful tug, thinking he had got hold of the maps but each time it was me he had got hold of!'

No sooner had Sam completed his tale of woe than out came Doc Theron, drying his hands on a towel.

'Now look here, you fellows,' he said, 'as far as I can make out you have had these things up inside you for about eighteen hours and during that time you have been bumping about in railway carriages and the truth is that if they were placed in the anal canal they may be anywhere now!'

Not very reassuring, and I had visions of going about for the rest of my days carrying a set of maps of the Ruhr about with me. However, Theron gave us some advice as to what immediate steps to take and this was to go to the lavatory and attempt to have a 'motion'. If all went well and the package was not seriously displaced, it would come out in the normal manner.

Oflag XII-B from the village.

The truss visible under the pullover.
March 1944.

I decided to put this into practice at once and repaired to 'abort' taking with me a large sheet of paper. I reckoned that having come this far it would be a pity to lose the precious maps down the pan. So I did my painful business in the corner on the paper and mercifully I was safely 'delivered'. Chutney and Sam had similar good fortune and this is how Oflag XII-B became the possessors of a complete set of War Office maps of the whole of Germany.

17th March 1944
A photograph of me has been taken in this camp. I am whiter and have lost some hair.

18th March 1944
Now, after fourteen days in this camp, our heavy kit has still not turned up and we are having to carry on with what we brought with us. In this camp there are one hundred and forty South Africans, thirty New Zealanders, fifteen Australians and about ninety English.

The building is a fairly modern (1910) convent: castle-like in shape, on a hill above the village. Central heating, no stoves, far more modern in all respects than our past home. Enough room to have one-sitting meals. The change, I feel, will be for the better. New faces, new ways, different cooking, etc. Our room is No. 25B; twelve officers (six English, three South Africans and three New Zealanders).[2] Most pleasant and reasonably roomy and comfortable.

I have taken greatly to natural history and the conditions of our last camp were perfect. I have stopped doing embroidery now for some few weeks but may resume if the cottons come my way in my next parcel.

24th March 1944
This place certainly gets the air raids! Nearly every day and night we hear or see our planes. The SBO is Brigadier Mountain and there is one other here, Brigadier Stebbings. Most of the officers are of senior rank and those that are not are rather OLD. It is definitely an old man's camp. There does not seem much vitality. Two generals visited the camp the day before yesterday. I am taking over the laundry of the camp – gives me something to do. Our luggage has still not arrived! Will it ever now?

28th March 1944
Today Angus-Leppan (South African) who died suddenly of heart failure on 26th was buried. I only knew him by sight. Memorial service at 12 noon. A Union Jack was painted on a sheet.[3]

International Prisoners of War medal with barbed wire.

<u>31st March 1944</u>
Weather warmer but have had a terrible cold. I play ping-pong every day and am improving rapidly. Our luggage has arrived at last after ONE MONTH! God bless Mrs Hamson for her lovely Xmas parcel which followed me here.

<u>7th April 1944</u>
Went to see the Medical Officer Farquhar about my hernia. He was not too encouraging. He said that the 'canal' has completely collapsed on the left side and is about to collapse on the right, and that 'surgical repair' is necessary.[4] The truss, although stopping it from getting any worse, is doing it no good (which I knew). At his instruction, I saw the German medical officer. He confirmed all that had been told me and put me down on the list to go to Limburg Hospital to be operated on, as soon as the ONE bed reserved for officers is free! So there it is. We must now await developments and I have been stopped ALL exercise. I shall miss my running in the morning.

The days pass and I am getting quickly into a groove – still hard at work at Spanish. Plenty of air activity to keep our spirits up. New restrictions have been imposed about the drawing of tins from the store. In many ways this camp cannot compare to IX-A but in some it is better. Our windows, which are about four yards from ground level, have been barb-wired, so that the rather indifferent view has been rendered positively loathsome! The Germans do not realise the hours we spend looking at the free world outside. Barbed wire becomes a 'phobia' after a time.

<u>17th April 1944</u>
Sixteen officers left today for Bad Soden[5] to see the Repatriation Board.

<u>19th April 1944</u>
Air attack. Limburg. Light bombing by American planes in daylight.

<u>21st April 1944</u>
They returned today. Five of them have passed, including, ironically enough, Gordon Brown who was shot here by one of the sentries in almost the exact circumstances of old Jones at Lübeck, the only difference being he did not get four bullets from a machine gun in the back, but one from a rifle in the shoulder. The sentry missed him (at about twenty yards!) with his first shot but got him with the second. He was standing right in the MIDDLE of the parade ground! As I have remarked elsewhere in this diary, nice people!

I had a very narrow escape myself the other day; while watching our bombers I stumbled over the tripwire and cut my leg quite badly – lucky

Hadamar Euthanasia Centre, taken from Oflag XII-B. The same church
is in both photographs and shows how close the camp was to the Centre,
where over 14,000 people were killed.

Major 'Joe' Johansen.

not to have fallen backwards over the wire or I should have been 'Gordon-Browned'! Limburg was bombed today. We could see it clearly from here. I am still waiting to go there to be operated on but my priority does not rank very high at present. On 18th we had a big Gestapo search.[6] About forty civilians were here from 8.30 am till 12.30 pm. No breakfast for us, as we were kept outside the building all the morning. Life drags on. There is a big rumour that eleven generals are coming here and the Germans have instructed us to clear the rooms for them. We are now awaiting developments. No news of operation yet.

5th May 1944

On 3rd the first of my swallowtail butterflies hatched – a beautiful specimen. It shed its skin after forty days of the most interesting performances in natural history. I had brought three chrysalises with me from Spangenberg. I am mounting this specimen and giving it to Johansen, one of the New Zealanders in our room, for his son.

Five officers left today for the 'holiday camp' in Bavaria![7] This is the same business as the Berlin one last year.

Had a very bad night last night with toothache and today Brigadier Stebbings (who in civilian life is a dentist) pulled one out for me. My face is still pretty swollen. I am to see him again on Monday.

No news yet of the generals coming. We are all to be X-rayed today for TB – they are bringing a portable machine. Have been told that I am to be operated on in three to four weeks. Inspection of camp by German General. Weather warm and sunny.

12th May 1944

Still in the hands of the dentist who is busy killing a nerve. Exceedingly painful. The X-ray was carried out quickly and efficiently. Four letters from Menda recently. The feeling about when the war will end remains about the same, some say two weeks, some say two months – others two years!

19th May 1944

German General inspected the camp yesterday. British generals not arrived yet – they now say Tuesday. Weather warmer. No letter from Joyce since 21st March. The Germans are now sending two of the orderlies to the Irish Camp![8] The holiday campers are due back next week. Have put in an application to leave this camp and to move to any other in Germany. The change from IX-A/H was NOT for the better. Many reasons cause me to say this, most of them cannot be entered in this book.[9]

With General Fortune, May 1944.

Fuck You Jack, I'm Alright.
135 x 135 mm

15. THE ETERNAL QUESTION

25th May 1944

General Fortune and ALL the brigadiers from Spangers[1] and Rotenburg have now arrived in this camp! It may improve now – I wonder. Five of them arrived on 23rd and General Fortune and the others yesterday. Protecting Power paid the usual visit today. Had my clothing parcel, five tobacco parcels and a Spanish dictionary today – exceptionally good day – all very welcome – I certainly am having some luck with parcels.

My application to leave this camp, with which I am quite thoroughly browned off,[2] has been turned down by the German General commanding prisoners of war. I only have one more visit to do at the dentist. Whatever else I may say or think about this camp, it certainly has given me the chance to have my teeth attended to, which means a very great deal. General Fortune has asked me to be his private secretary and look after all his private and official mail, other than that which concerns this camp. Naturally, I accepted. It will be interesting and I take it as a compliment.

28th May 1944

The dress in this camp, which has been exceedingly SLOPPY both on parade and off, has now been brought up to IX-A/H standards![3] It has shaken quite a few of them.

Very heavy air activity. Limburg bombed again, could be seen very clearly from this camp. Light bombing by American planes in daylight. Not quite so keen on being operated on in Limburg now! Not only the bombing, but six cases of tetanus died while Pop Torr was there – something to do with bad gut – all post-operational!

29th May 1944

Hadamar machine-gunned today by two Allied fighters; hundreds of bombers over as well. A few bombs behind the camp in daylight and also in Niederhadamar – a very exciting day.

1st June 1944

Three years ago today! How much longer will it be, is the eternal question. Hope to finish with the dentist very soon. I am taking NO exercise these days, the swelling is bigger but not much. The German potato ration is now fifty-six per cent uneatable. This figure was arrived at over an average of the last few days. They had stored badly and more than half are rotten. Complaints have been made and the Germans are very sorry but nothing can be done.

6th June 1944
News of the INVASION today. Everyone terrifically excited![4]

9th June 1944
Now that the invasion has really started and now that the Italian front is moving, we are all very optimistic – maybe over-optimistic. Being students of the German Press, as we are forced to be, it is very interesting to hear all about the invasion, as for the last three years we have been promised that any attacking force would be thrown back into the sea!

Two officers who escaped from the holiday camp, Lt Colonel Blake (South Africa, DSO) and Maxwell (Fifth Fusiliers),[5] are now back here again, in the cooler. I hardly feel I want to be operated on here now that things are moving – anyway there has been no news. My February parcel arrived yesterday and as usual contained the most lovely things, too lovely for our filthy, depressing surroundings.

16th June 1944
A hole has been discovered in the showers, which has resulted in them being closed indefinitely. Big search of our room on 12th. It took me two hours to put all my kit straight. Weather very cold and wet. Life goes on and we are all very optimistic. Mail very slow from home, which is only to be expected these days.

17th June 1944
So relieved that I am free from ceaseless toothache. Very lucky to find the facilities here to have my mouth put right. I only hope that for some time I will be clear now. I found salt cleaned them up well. It's a useful tip to know.

23rd June 1944
Three officers, Saleby, Nichol and Jones, have arrived after being at large for seven months in Italy! Nichol is RA. Prior to going into hospital I am to be inoculated against tetanus, I have arranged that much, but no news of going in. Jumbo McLeod has come back from the holiday camp but is in the cooler for having money found on him. He has got seven days! Nice rest cure. Would willingly swop with him. David Lumsden (Black Watch) has arrived from Spangers. Weather still cold and horrible. Still no showers; the hole in the floor is not yet mended.

25th June 1944

Inspection by German General. Complaints made that we have not had a bath for over three weeks.

29th June 1944

The German High Command have posted a notice on the board that, owing to the 'bombing of residential areas' and the 'machine-gunning of civilians', the civilians 'may find expression' of this in their attitude towards us. No comment necessary.

7th July 1944

A transit camp has now been opened in Hadamar for officers. So far there are thirty-one officers and other ranks from the invasion, mostly parachutists and airborne troops. We are, of course, allowed no contact with them, but we have sent them food and clothing. The Senior British Officer is Lord Cranleigh. We understand they are very optimistic. Inspection yesterday by German officers. Weather wet.

14th July 1944

Big Gestapo search on 12th, with the usual result that we had no breakfast until 11.30 am.

This searching business gets very tiring after three years. Everything you have, letters, etc., all gone through and turned upside down. Some of them are reasonably careful, others intentionally the reverse. The main rooms were so badly knocked about in this search that the General had the Camp Germans up to inspect it.

I am due for hospital in about a month from now – at least so they say. I think I shall go in spite of everything, as the temptation is very great to be quite fit when I do get home. I hear from Cairo that General Kaffatos is now at X-B[6] in the north, so that he has had a move too. I am glad Mum is still sending him parcels.

17th July 1944

Managed to get a new palliasse[7] and have it filled with new wood shavings. The old one was intolerable. Now it feels as though I have a feather mattress!

20th July 1944

Yesterday bombs dropped very near here and the whistling as they came down reminded everyone of old times! Very heavy air raids by day. The war drags on and, naturally, we are impatient.

Yacht from a drawing by Major 'Joe' Johansen.
110 x 150 mm

<u>21st July 1944</u>
Attempt on Hitler's life.[8] Himmler is now the General Officer Commanding all the German troops in Germany![9]

<u>24th July 1944</u>
Army salute now substituted for the Nazi salute by the German Army, which all the German officers in the camp have now adopted. They seem very self-conscious!!

<u>28th July 1944</u>
Am seeing the German doctor today about my operation. The Protecting Power come tomorrow.

Still studying Spanish, which comes very easy to me now.

Mail a little better. Red Cross parcels are beginning to give out and we now only get one every ten days. When we get a parcel a week, we are not conscious of food and hunger but as soon as this slender thread is broken, then we get pretty worried as we all know what it is to be hungry. There are only three more issues left. German rations have been cut by two hundred and twenty grains[10] per week per head of barley, and millet replaced by potatoes which have already been estimated at over sixty per cent bad and are even worse now. Getting hungry again.

<u>4th August 1944</u>
I have now been told definitely that NO operations can now be done unless urgent, so I am back again where I started with no chance of being put right – they might just as well have told me so in the first place instead of raising hopes. Inspection yesterday by German General from OKW.

<u>11th August 1944</u>
Saw Medical Officer again today and he examined me. He says I have a 'direct' rupture on both sides and must be careful. Since Monday 8th have had quite a lot of spare time and sitting in the sun. We are luckily on a fine spell. The second lot of holiday campers have returned – personally, I would not go if I was paid – I ask no favours from the Germans.

Parcels have arrived and we are back again to normal food after being on 'short commons'.[11]

<u>12th August 1944</u>
The weather is delightful now. I lie stripped in underpants and roast! Sunbathing undoubtedly causes the days to fly.

Cartoon of the incident of 13 September 1944,
by Major Morris, 7th Ghurkas.

<u>18th August 1944</u>
We are on a very fine hot spell of weather – am very sunburnt. I am taking Cervantes courageously. Have started some extracts from 'Don Q.'[12] in Spanish; rather difficult, but I have just read through the whole book in English which helps.

Plenty of parcels now, the bulk from the Argentine. Still doing a bit of embroidery. Everyone very optimistic these days – I seem to take a longer view than most people! No news from Menda for ages. Hope she is still well.

<u>20th August 1944</u>
I sometimes feel I am not deserving of everyone's kindness – one feels quite useless. Perhaps one may not be afterwards.

<u>25th August 1944</u>
Weather still very fine. No news from Joyce since early June. Colonel Waddilove (AQMG to Brigadier Tilney on Leros) has arrived from VIII-F[13] where he was Senior British Officer. I play ping-pong every evening and have got hold of the game well now.

<u>1st September 1944</u>
The fine weather is over and all the ping-pong balls are broken so even that little bit of exercise has gone. For reasons of my own I have destroyed my parole card and refuse to go on any more walks or give my parole again to the Germans. I am sorry I ever did in the first place. Anyway, I am quite satisfied to remain behind the wire until the end of the war. Have been busy the last few days with the General's letters. Our Royal Marines, four of them, are leaving for the Marlag[14] today. On 27th August five rapatriés[15] (Caliston, Perry, G-Brown, Mair and McInnes) actually left here for England!

<u>5th September 1944</u>
Daylight attack on Limburg airport by Allied dive-bombers.

<u>6th September 1944</u>
Have almost completely finished my silks – I might carry on maybe for two weeks yet. The parcel containing more may come, I hope, fairly soon.

<u>7th September 1944</u>
Brigadier Stewart, NZEF,[16] has just arrived from Italy – captured on 1st August. Every day we have signs here that we are getting near the battle zone, or rather that the battle is coming our way.

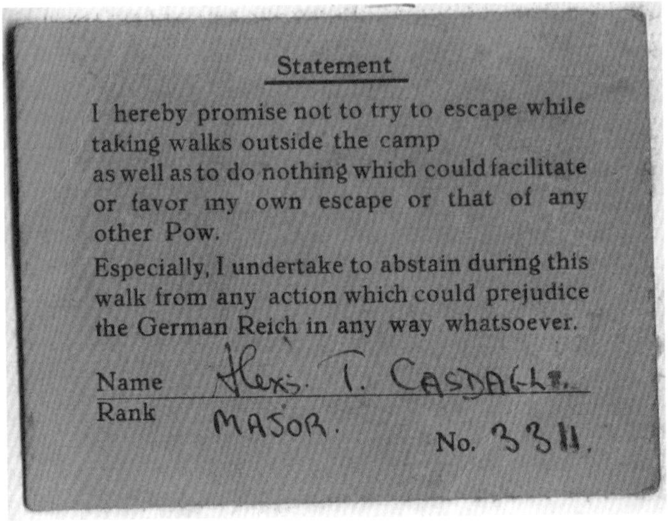
Statement

I hereby promise not to try to escape while taking walks outside the camp as well as to do nothing which could facilitate or favor my own escape or that of any other Pow.

Especially, I undertake to abstain during this walk from any action which could prejudice the German Reich in any way whatsoever.

Name Alexis T. Casdagli.
Rank Major. No. 3311.

Parole card, Oflag XII-B.

15th September 1944

The terrific air activity of the last few days is now dying down; we can see Limburg aerodrome being bombed and machine-gunned. An American plane dropped three ammunition belts in the camp. One hit the wall just outside our window; presumably he was hit and lightening his plane.

We feel the war quite near these days. The love-campers[17] have returned, including Brigadier Parrington who had been Senior British Officer there. I was very pleased to see him again.[18] Brigadier Clifton, NZEF,[19] is taking his place.

19th September 1944

Heavy daylight bombing. Four waves of American bombers. One's mind becomes quite chaotic: I never thought the war would last into its sixth year for instance! It will be over someday I suppose. The curious thing is almost everyone, I find, reckoned to be free almost immediately! The saving factor is to have faith.[20]

Consolidated B-24 Liberator.

Flying Fortresses also known as Boeing B-17s.

16. PORTRAIT OF A PRISONER

<u>22nd September 1944</u>

Many heavy air raids these days – we had a ringside seat for the Limburg bombing of 19th. Five waves went over: pretty horrible really to watch in cold blood. Regularly now we see fleets of seven hundred to one thousand (counted!) Flying Fortresses and Liberators[1] droning overhead, with busy little fighters, incredibly high, humming about like gnats.[2]

We now have an air raid shelter and ARP regulation that says 'escaping is no longer a sport!' Everyone to be shot at sight, etc. The accompanying order (No. 254) dated 22nd September 1944 reads: 'There were found with British troops books, edited by the British High Command, with instructions ordering British troops to employ in their warfare the methods of gangsters, methods which up to now were used by the American underworld but not by soldiers conscious of their honour. This induced the German High Command to take countermeasures. These refer also to escapes of prisoners of war. For further particulars see the posters which are to be posted up by order of OKW. In observance of this order I direct to stick up one poster each on the notice board, in the music room, in the dining room, in the ballroom as well as in the Transit Camp. It is not allowed to take off these posters.' It is signed by Lapp, Oberst und Kommandant.[3]

Here is what the poster says:

TO ALL PRISONERS OF WAR
The escape from prison camps is no longer a sport!

Germany has always kept to the Hague Convention,[4] only punishing recaptured prisoners of war with minor disciplinary punishment. Germany will still maintain these principles of International Law. But England besides fighting at the front in an honest manner has instituted an illegal warfare in non-combat zones in the form of gangster commandos, terror bandits and sabotage troops even up to the frontiers of Germany. They say in a captured and secret confidential English military pamphlet:

The Handbook of Modern Irregular Warfare
'The days when we could practise the rules of sportsmanship are over.

Catherine Casdagli, mother.

For the time being every soldier must be a potential gangster and must be prepared to adopt these methods whenever necessary. The sphere of operations should always include the enemy's own territory, any occupied territory and, in certain circumstances, such neutral countries as he is using as a source of supply.'

England has with these instructions opened up a non-military form of gangster war! Germany is determined to safeguard her homeland and especially her war industry and principal centres for the fighting fronts. Therefore it has been necessary to create strictly forbidden zones, called death zones, in which all unauthorised trespassers will be immediately shot on sight. Escaping POWs entering such death zones will certainly lose their lives. They are therefore in constant danger of being mistaken for enemy agents or sabotage groups.
Urgent warning is given against making futures escapes!
In plain English: Stay in the camp where you will be safe! Breaking out of it now is a damned dangerous act.
The chances of preserving your life are almost nil!
All military and police guards have been given the most strict orders to shoot at sight all suspected persons.

'Escaping from prison camps has ceased to be a sport!'

27th September 1944
Parcels now every fortnight. This is an instruction from Geneva and I do not suppose we shall ever get back to one a week. We can appreciate the difficulties of supply. No letters for weeks, no private parcels for months. The war gets closer and more audible daily.

29th September 1944
Mum is in touch with General Kaffatos and I am very glad. It means a lot to me, as I have a very high regard for him. Foreign Office man here today.

Much air activity. Fighters fly at 0 feet over the camp. We see thousands of bombers and fighters machine-gunning. V-1 emplacements are quite near and we can see and hear the famous secret weapon in action.[5] Everything is in a great state of excitement – very disturbing but I manage to keep my Spanish going regularly.

Brigadier Clifton has now gone as Senior British Officer to the Love Camp, which they are still keeping open apparently.[6]

Two-mark note.

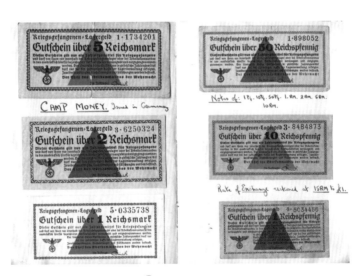

Camp money.

<u>30th September 1944</u>

All our camp money was withdrawn today and in its place were given us real German marks! They really are an extraordinary nation! For the last four years they have been doing all they can to prevent us from having real money and putting people in the cooler for having it, etc., and now they dish it out to us in as many thousands as our credit is good for. Amazing! The transit camp have sent away forty-five men and refilled up with another hundred.

<u>8th October 1944</u>

Captain Micklethwait, RN,[7] has arrived here from VIII-F. They are certainly having an exciting time there – rather too exciting! Several officers have been killed, among them Lt Colonel Kilkelly (8th Hussars)[8] – fancy, I never knew that Smash was in Germany and now he has been killed here – what a waste! Parcels every fourteen days, makes one pretty hungry and, with the colder weather coming on, I am personally ravenous! Letters and private parcels almost at a standstill. Only to be expected.

<u>13th October 1944</u>

The next repatriation party have left for Bad Soden to see the Board and are due back tomorrow. I have just worked out that, had I gone to Limburg for my operation as expected, I would have been there on 19th September and as the hospital was HIT, I consider myself lucky. Inspection today by the SS Obergruppenführer![9] German money has now been called IN again! Now we have NO money – camp or real – and everything is to be done by chits. We spend very little anyway.

<u>15th October 1944</u>

Limburg. Light daylight bombing by American planes.

<u>17th October 1944</u>

I have felt very close to Mum these last years, not only by being able to write but being able to appreciate her sufferings.

<u>20th October 1944</u>

Another cut in the bread ration by two hundred and twenty-five grains per week and an increase in potatoes of six hundred grains. Am very, very hungry these days. We have been on half parcel a week for two months now. The colder weather makes it worse. Have not been consistently hungry since Lübeck days. We do not realise how well off we are until parcels fail and rations are cut. Personally I do not think any more parcels will get through,

Casdagli's fork.

Casdagli's knife.

A. T. Casdagli by Earl Haig. Oil on board.
240 x 370 mm

and I am no longer very hopeful of seeing the war over in 1944. I go to sleep dreaming of food and every book one reads seems to be full of descriptions of exotic meals. All the old symptoms of 1941 coming back.

On 18th October a petrol tank was dropped just five yards from the wire of this camp by one of our fighters – very exciting. Amazing how things keep on dropping round here. Today was overshadowed by the sad and sudden death of Ian McConnell Wood, who died just outside our window having come back from the sports ground. Very sad, he leaves a wife and four children – I liked him very much.

23rd October 1944

Funeral today of Ian McConnell Wood. What a wonderful way to die, when all is said and done. Just like a candle. He died of heart failure. Sad all the same.

29th October 1944

Weather very cold. Frost last night. We are all very, very hungry these days and the cut in the bread ration is making itself felt. We get a few more potatoes but they are already starting to go bad. A few private parcels came in but no Red Cross. Things look pretty bad as regards food but we shall get used to it.

9th November 1944

Still hungry and very cold. The central heating in this building is very indifferent. Buchan, Clemens and Fell all had blackouts today – partly cold and partly food. Personally I am keeping well. There are a lot of 'malades imaginaires'[10] about! In five days' hard reading, I have just finished the complete 'War and Peace' – thirteen hundred and fifty-two large pages – not bad going and no one here has done it in less. Thoroughly enjoyed every word of it, although frankly the second epilogue was a bit beyond me.[11] Head man of all prisoners of war in Germany, Lt Gen. Newman,[12] and Earl Haig (Capt., Scots Greys) have been moved to another camp. The portrait Earl Haig painted of me (which he has since let me have) was much admired in the recent exhibition: he is a nice young lad.[13]

MAIL.

OUTWARD.

1·6 – 31·5.

		1941.	1942.	1943.	1944.
LETTERS.	General.	13.	49.	45	39
..	Home	12.	24.	36	32
P.C.	General.	20.	-	-	4
..	Home	15.	18	19	12
Printed Cards.		26.	45.	32	-
Red + Messages.		1.	2.	1.	-

TOTAL : 92. 138. 133. 87.

INWARD.

		1941.	1942.	1943.	1944.
LETTERS . CARDS.	General.	105.	147.	117.	55.
..	Home.	40.	46.	38.	17.

TOTAL. 145. 193. 155. 72.

Record of mail.

17. PUT ME IN THE COOLER

10th November 1944
Limburg. Fighter-bomber attack on aerodrome.

11th November 1944
Visit of Protecting Power. Not much hope of parcels. Armistice Day service as usual today. Filthy weather. Heaters are now working but only indifferently. Life not quite so miserable – this camp really is a shocker!

14th November 1944
Have again started growing my moustache!

22nd November 1944
Visit of International Red Cross yesterday. Had an interview to see what they can do about Menda – they will send her a message from me. German General visited the camp today. Very wet and unpleasant. We hear gunfire clearly and regularly now in the west, all day every day. Still very hungry. Almost getting used to it, as one does, little by little. General Fortune is still in hospital where he has been for the past few months.[1] I see him about once a week – he seems better these days. Walks again stopped for 'undisciplined behaviour'. It does not worry me because I do not go. How glad I am I stopped giving my parole. You know where you are!

25th November 1944
Hadamar. A few bombs dropped locally. Destination unknown.

26th November 1944
Great excitement today. Allied dive-bombers came and bombed and machine-gunned a train just outside Hadamar station. Very clear weather – had a perfect view as the east side of this camp directly overlooks Hadamar station. The building shook, some plaster came down in Room 82. More V-2s[2] clearly visible – fascinating to watch. Attack on military train by fighter-bombers at Niederhadamar. Gunfire all day.

29th November 1944
Hadamar. Attack on passenger train just outside station. The engine was damaged. I again had a perfect view. We saw it being towed in.

4th December 1944
Hadamar. A few bombs locally – one near Galgenberg. Very loud.

11th December 1944
Further excitement these days. Limburg. Daylight raid through cloud. One stick of bombs and then later several sticks through cloud on the autobahn.[3] We hear very loud gunfire now; the windows are continually rattling. Food is very short and we get our last and final parcel on 15th December. Fortunately I have drawn a Canadian one of which there are a few left. The odds were ten to one against. After that, German rations! Snow and cold. Am losing weight – otherwise fit.

12th December 1944
Limburg. Dive-bombing and machine-gunning of northeast part of the town and skyline.

22nd December 1944
Life drags on in the midst of the German counter-attack which has rather put the optimists in the shade these days. We do not hear the gunfire now as we used to do! The horrors of an 'organised' camp Xmas are approaching – truly awful. I am ALL against it and only want to be left alone! Many others feel as I do. They say there is an Xmas meal in store for us. The camp, through the Senior British Officer, has given its parole for the period 4.30 pm 24th December till 8.30 am 26th December. In MY opinion this is a very wrong action and although it was done here last year before we arrived, it is none the less a precedent that has not been present in any other camp in Germany in all these years. In my opinion it is wrong because it is being done solely for our comfort (which is NOT one of the reasons sanctioned by the War Office); secondly, the Germans can reduce their guards for this period and are free from responsibility of our escaping; we should keep them at full pressure at all times.

I went to the Executive Officer, Lt Colonel Allan Spowers (DSO, MC, 24th Battalion Australian Imperial Force) and lodged a protest saying that the action had been taken FOR the camp without asking them and that I personally would NOT give my parole. He said he would report it to the Senior British Officer.

Next morning I was summoned to Brigadier Eden (acting for General Fortune who is still ill) and stated my case. After a lot of talk he said that I could not stand out from this 'mass parole' and that it was his 'DIRECT ORDER' that I give my parole – an order I was bound to obey but in my own mind I am not at all sure that it was an order that he is entitled to give me. In fact, my parole is being given 'on compulsion'. I argued that I should be put in the cooler for the period, so that the Germans would be satisfied that everyone else was 'on parole'. I begged him to do this but he refused saying that it would give the Germans the idea that we were having trouble among ourselves, which would no doubt please them. With this I felt bound to agree – but not before I went back a second time and asked him to reconsider his order, which he refused to do. Although others I spoke to FULLY AGREE with my view and my ACTION, only one, Baty (Major RTR), had the GUTS to do the same – so the laissez-faire spirit wins again – it is ABSOLUTELY INFURIATING. What can the action of two people do out of two hundred and sixty – had fifty or sixty gone, he would have HAD to change his orders and NOT give parole for the camp. My VIEWS are very STRONG on this.

23rd December 1944
Night bombing of Limburg at 6.30 pm with several heavy calibre bombs which shook the building; severe window rattling – actually one of our panes has been loosened. Stalag hit.[4] Bombs heard whistling down 9.30 pm. More bombs to the west.

26th December 1944
Had my best view so far of V-1s and V-2s being fired. In the beautiful clear sky it is fascinating to watch. Many rumours about last night's bombing but it seems clear the Stalag was hit: they say forty-eight officers were killed and two hundred other casualties – what a terrible tragedy for us.

Yesterday being Xmas day we had a really big meal in the evening and spent ALL day – quite literally ALL DAY in BED. Shall be pleased when we are back to normal.

31st December 1944
New Year's Eve and another year nearly gone – another year of my 'future' WASTED away. Brigadier Clifton now back from the Love Camp which has been permanently closed – he looks very fit – no wonder! Bridgeman (Captain RASC), who went to Limburg Hospital in a hurry to be operated on for a strangulated hernia, is back again after about eight weeks! He is very, very ill – his wound is septic and his nerves all to hell from the bombing. The hospital was hit again, the man in the next bed to him killed and the man the other side wounded. How lucky I have been not to be allowed to be operated on! Casualties are now said to be sixty to seventy officers killed at Limburg – mostly Americans.[5]

Emergency ration tin.

Oflag XII-B. Reading room. © ICRC

1st January 1945
Limburg. Bombs in daylight on aerodrome. Some behind Galgenberg at 1.20 pm. At 1.40 pm, bombs seen on Elz, about two and a half miles away. At 1.55 pm, bombs seen Limburg town area. Brilliant sunshine.

7th January 1945
The transit camp[6] were allowed to come up to a performance of our pantomime; actually it was Rupert Christie's of IX-A/H last year. Rupert is now here and again it went off very well. We were allowed no contact or intercourse with the transit boys; they all seemed young and fit and for the most part are the airborne Arnhem crowd.[7] They have an officer of theirs here in our cooler. He has been in five weeks or so – for writing in his letters that the Germans were 'bastards'.

Food fills our thoughts now. I find everyone talks about food and the old hunger of Lübeck days is back again: we have only had German rations since our parcel of 15th December finished. Am nice and slim. Very little to smoke too.

There was a close and heavy bombing of Elz and Limburg at 12.07 this morning. It was through cloud and we saw no planes but heard the bombs whistling down and six windows of ours were blown out, including the one under which I was sitting in the mess; luckily I had bobbed down – my table was covered in glass! The shockingly cold weather and already indifferent heating will make broken windows a real trial. I do not suppose these will be the last to be broken either. The official Stalag casualties from the German doctor are eighty-three American officers, four British officers and some Italian and French officers – all killed and one hundred wounded.

14th January 1945
Limburg. Heavy bombing and machine-gunning at 11.30 am. Sunshine.

15th January 1945
Stephenson, Wakely-Smith and Munro-Fraser have left for England – the latter took an embroidered belt home with him to give to Joyce. Weather very cold, much snow. Twice we have had over thirty-two degrees of frost F. Heaters only moderate; we feel the cold more having only German rations to eat. On Sunday our meat was a sheep which had been killed in last week's bombing of Elz! Pretty mangled stuff it was too! A lot of air activity lately and good view of V-1s and V-2s. No letters for ages. Spend a lot of time in bed trying to keep warm – no one even <u>walks</u> very much these days, in order not to work up an appetite. Three years ago I arrived at IX-A/H. How I wish I was back.

Old Harrovian Case.
Old Harrovian colours and the Wanderers colours. 143 x 45 mm

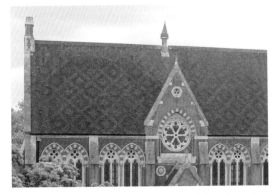

The roof of the Vaughan Library, Harrow School, with a similar
pattern to the *Old Harrovian Case.*

18. THE FLAP IS ON

22nd January 1945
We had a bit of shaking last night when eighteen of our windows were smashed by a large bomb dropped about 1,000 yards west of the camp and some plaster came down – it must have been the hell of a size! In this snowy, frosty weather it makes things pretty draughty particularly as the Germans have no more glass and wood: cardboard has to be used!

One hundred British parcels have been sent to us from the Stalag – it will come to one third to one quarter each, which will be a terrific event for us. It will not keep us going for long. Everyone losing a lot of weight rapidly on German rations – no wonder. I have taken my belt in another hole but feel well.

29th January 1945
Visit of International Red Cross today. Had an interview with them about Menda. They are doing all they can but the recent Greek troubles have not helped.[1] Have not had a word from Cairo for eight months. There are strong rumours of more food parcels coming for us from Limburg. I now weigh just ten stone, twelve lb thirteen oz. Weather continues very cold and frosty. Heaters are shockingly inadequate and the lighting and water fail regularly now as the result of the big raids in the district.

1st February 1945
The miracle has happened and two thousand and sixty American Red Cross food parcels have come for us; we are to get one a week for three weeks, the last of which will start the fourteen-day issues. This is terrific! Most people two to three stone down. My weight, given above, shows about two stones drop, but cannot say accurately. Some people have dropped as much as seven stone – (Lt Colonel McCarter, MC, AIF). We are now set up for a reasonable diet for two–three months, for which the Lord be praised. What a difference it has made to everyone.

2nd February 1945
Limburg. West of the town. Two planes machine-gunned a train in clear weather at 10.00 am – clouds of steam from the engine.

3rd February 1945
Limburg and district: fighter-bomber attack and machine-gunning. Very

clear, 2.40 pm. Very heavy raid last night to the south (Wiesbaden?), the biggest night raid I have yet seen. Fifty miles away I should say but truly terrifying, even from here!

6th February 1945
We are now without light or water or power, following the big raid on 3rd. Locomotives are watering in Hadamar all day long. Electric grid must be badly damaged.

8th February 1945
Lightnings[2] attacked Limburg, machine-gunning and a few bombs, 8.55 am. Sunshine. Lightnings machine-gunning and dive-bombing on Limburg at 3.30 pm. Heavy AA fire, also light Flak.[3] Fairly clear.

9th February 1945
Hadamar. Burst of machine-gun fire on the railway line near the station at 8.30 pm.

11th February 1945
Limburg. Lightnings attacked with bombs and machine guns. Clear weather. At 9.40 am fighter-bomber attack on targets between Limburg and Hadamar. Bombs near, also machine-gun fire, eight planes, at 9.40–10.30 am in various directions. Heavy bombs dropped on Limburg.

12th February 1945
The thaw has set in properly but we are back again with light, water and power, which is a blessing; we have to burn margarine when the current is off, as the Germans make NO provision. We all feel much better for our food. The average loss of weight has been estimated at thirty-one lb per head. Maximum ninety-four lb. Still no mail.

Am feeling particularly browned off mentally these days – it must be this camp – even my room is not a patch on the old Room 13 at XI-A/H. Here there is far too much bickering and squabbling – I keep out of it at ALL COSTS. Plenty of local air activity, bombing and machine-gunning. They have now brought quite a lot of heavy AA to Limburg, which makes quite a row and shakes our windows when they open up.

13th February 1945
Limburg. Lightnings attacked town at house top level at 2.43 pm. Light AA. Very clear.

14th February 1945
Limburg. Strong dive-bomber attack at 1.15 pm. Clear. Many bombs. Lightnings also drop a few bombs in woods west of camp at 1.55 pm.

17th February 1945
Air activity continues hot and strong, day and night. On 14th the newly arrived AA drew its first blood when it shot down one of the American four-engined bombers. We saw it all clearly; it did not catch fire but just tumbled out of the sky and crashed. Rather a horrible sight to see, really, we hope the crew baled out. We were weighed again yesterday and I have gained one lb in the fortnight of food, others have gained as much as seven lb and some have shown no change. Dobson had a belated private parcel and found it had been shot up by our own aircraft – the whole thing was riddled – no wonder ours are not coming through!

21st February 1945
East of Hadamar at 11.30 am fighter attack. Very close. Dive-bombing attack on Limburg at 12.50 pm. Several bombs and machine-gunning.

23rd February 1945
Fighter-bomber attack on Limburg at 3.35 p.m. Cannon fire. Big flash and large mushrooms of smoke followed one dive – ammunition? Clear.

24th February 1945
Fighter-bomber attack on Limburg road and railway at 9.50–10.00 am. No heating whatever in the building now! Poor Paul van der Gucht (Indian Army, Ordnance Corps) was taken off by ambulance to Limburg last night – seriously ill – stomach trouble – an operation necessary. The Germans have started to placard the place with anti-Russian propaganda – rather late in the day! Limburg and Hadamar had machine-gunning on railway from 10.20 p.m. onwards.

27th February 1945
Paul has been operated on and going on well. Alan McClure, his stepfather, is in touch with him. Five hundred grains per head per week cut in potatoes! Cold and wet. Went to Brigadier Stebbings, the dentist, today and I was passed with nothing to be done – I am delighted.

2nd March 1945
Fighter-bomber attack at 3.55 pm. Two planes, one bomb. One bomb dropped at 4.30 am from a single plane.

5th March 1945
Hadamar. Three fighters attacked railway north of the town. Bombs seen at
1.10 pm. Machine-gunning on the railway at 8.50 pm.

8th March 1945
Hadamar, to the east, at 2.15 pm. Planes dropped bombs over the hill opposite
our eastern windows: bombing preceded by bomb signal. Very clear.

9th March 1945
Fighter-bomber attacks, Limburg area, at 2.25 pm. Cloudy. East of Hadamar
fighter-bomber attacks between 3.00 and 3.30 pm. Machine-gunning too.

10th March 1945
Everyone in a great flap these days as the war gets nearer and the possibilities
of a move loom larger. Bridgeman has been moved back to Limburg Hospital,
and Paul, who was to have come back, is being kept there. This makes us
think that we shall move, if they can possibly do it. I personally have arranged
and re-sorted all my kit. Day and night now we see and hear our planes, it
is now the exception not to. The Stalag was hit again on 9th and six French
and three Germans were killed – they certainly are having a miserable time.

11th March 1945
Heavy bombing through cloud behind Galgenberg at 11.35 am.

12th March 1945
The move flap is dying down but it is a very present possibility. We have
drawn out all our reserve tins of food and tobacco rather than leave them here
in the event of a hurried move. A notice by the Commandant says that a move
may come and that we shall be 'quite certainly' under martial law when on
the move and must 'adapt our conduct accordingly'. We saw a German fighter
crash today – a mile or two from the camp; the pilot baled out and landed
safely; the plane came from the west, obviously hit – the war is very near now.

13th March 1945
Hadamar. Sustained air activity by American fighter-bombers from 2.45 to
3.45 pm. Many targets attacked. Repeated widespread local activity from
5.30 to 6.30 pm.

14th March 1945
General Fortune left yesterday with Mack, his servant, for Limburg Hospital;

from which we are glad to hear that his repatriation is being arranged on an exchange basis.[4] I am very glad as he has had a rotten time.

The Swiss arrived today on their usual visit.

Terrific air activity these days in the brilliant weather – culminating in a fighter-bomber attack on Hadamar railway station at 5.25 pm. Four planes with bombs and machine-gun fire. Ninety-seven windows are broken in the building, including seven in our room, and the whole place pretty well shaken by the bombs and cannon fire. Terrific noise. There is no Ack Ack here and the attack was from a very low level. Arthur Wood slightly cut on the head by falling glass. Some damage at the station, some casualties from machine-gunning and bombing. We shall be 'camping out' indefinitely now as there is no possible chance of having the glass replaced – and would it be worth it?

I took advantage of the fine weather today to do a test walk and walked solidly from 8.05 am till the bombing at 5.30 pm – eight hours with intervals for meals. I averaged about three miles per hour. Not a bad effort as I have hardly walked at all; feet and thighs rather sore and tired.

15th March 1945
Inoculated against typhus today. There is an outbreak in the Limburg Stalag. After effects not too bad: rather a headache. The brilliant weather continues and with it incessant air activity.

16th March 1945
Dive-bombing and machine-gunning at 9.30–10.00 am. Misty. Fighter-bombers over town area at 1.15 pm. Machine-gunning by fighter-bombers over town area at 4.15 pm.

We have now been told that we are to move by rail! None of us looking forward to it very much! Sometime next week they say. Everyone in a bit of a flap. Terrific air activity continues. The war is getting very near us and we hate the idea of moving.

17th March 1945
Another heavy attack by fighter-bombers on Hadamar station. Two direct hits on the crossing, two other hits on the track – much damage – rails all over the place. No one hurt. Six more windows blown and most of the cardboard: total now one hundred and twenty-seven windows. I was up in one of the towers at 3.20 pm, the time of the attack, and saw it all from there. The transit camp buildings were blown in and the camp is closed down. Twelve officers and nine OR have come up here this evening! We are wondering when and how the move will take place now.

Magic Square with an Oflag number on each side.
100 x 100 mm

18th March 1945

Another local attack at 1.15 pm. A few bombs on Niederhadamar and Hadamar. We now go down to the shelters, or rather the basement of the building – we certainly are getting the fireworks these days! Gangs are busy trying to repair the track. Very exciting talking to all the new officers, some only one month old! An order has been given that we are to leave at 1.00 am tomorrow, probably by road transport. Everyone is ready packed – then comes a cancellation of the order at 10.30 pm! The flap is on.

19th March 1945

Same order given that we should leave from here tonight by lorry – we were on half-hour's notice after dark. No move took place.

20th March 1945

Great air activity continues. Today we were again on half-hour's notice after dark. We actually paraded and stood about four hours in the cold night and eventually only eighty officers moved. Very tiring and upsetting.

21st March 1945

Same intense air activity by day and night. All our kit which we cannot carry is now in the greenhouse – labelled to the War Office! This evening what was left of the camp paraded again for the move to Lollar, north of Giessen. We were kept waiting from 7.20 pm till 11.20 pm as Brigadier Clifton was missing![5] Eventually moved, fifty standing in a truck with all our kit. We left Hadamar after midnight.[6]

LIBERATION

'Tin-bashed' mug, with initials 'ATC'.

19. THE AMERICANS ARE COMING

<u>22nd March 1945</u>

We arrived at Lollar at 4.30 am after passing through Weilburg, Wetzlar and Giessen, a journey of forty miles: the last named being a scene of devastation which in the moonlight was positively ghastly – fires still burning.

Eventually we were settled down in a foreign workers' camp near the railway and joined to a munition factory, which has been out of production some time. We are accommodated in huts, sleeping on the concrete, forty to a room – the all time LOW. Terribly tired and fell asleep at once. We are all very cheerful. Spent all day here, no move further east, although we are told this is not our final destination. Terrific air activity all day. No casualties but some very near bombing and machine-gunning of railway at Lollar, which is only five to six hundred yards from our huts. We are making the best of very bad conditions. German rations (bread and sausage) are being issued.

<u>23rd March 1945</u>

Still no move – all the railway lines from here appear to be damaged – there is talk of us going to Fulda by train or by lorry to Spangenberg! The war appears to be going very well and the Germans are certainly hard put to it to move us. Have now joined forces with Joe Johansen and we share a bit of straw and floor space and also all our food – could not hope to be with a better companion under these conditions. A little less air activity today but some oil bombs were dropped on the railway by Lightnings – quite near us – excellent view.

<u>24th March 1945</u>

Not expected to move now before Monday. Everyone shaking down to some sort of order in this place. We have put out white 'POW' signs on the ground and we <u>think</u> that the USAAC know all about us, but some of their good targets are pretty close! One sixth of a Red Cross parcel (which we brought with us) issued today. No move yet. Saw many heavies[1] and there was fairly consistent fighter activity near us. We have a service of a few minutes in the evenings, roll call 7.30 am and 6.30 pm, which makes a very long day. Germans still issue food.

<u>25th March 1945</u>

Palm Sunday! Roll call at 8.00 am which synchronised with a low-level attack on the station by Thunderbolts.[2] As we are in huts in a field and not more than six hundred yards from the line, people were a little 'unsteady' on parade. The bombs could be seen actually dropping, plenty of machine-gunning too. It was reassuring that the planes gave us no personal attention.

At 1.00 pm sensational attack on the railway by Lightnings – very low, oil bombs dropped and cannon fire. Several tracks set on fire. No sign of a move yet. Another glorious day of perfect weather ended! A move becomes less and less likely and we do not mind staying here.

26th March 1945

No question of a move from this area now. We are told we may move a 'short distance' to other 'safer billets'. Clouds and rain till the afternoon, no air capacity till it cleared. Small parties seen moving from the south, either prisoners of war, foreign workers, or refugees: all heading north on foot. Fighter-bombers active to the south and an enormous fire away to the southeast. Air activity only in the evening. The war gets closer – we can certainly <u>hear</u> it! – and rumours are flying round.

27th March 1945

We were told at 11.45 am today that the German Commandant has handed over the camp to us and considered the war lost for Germany. The guard have been withdrawn: we were told we were no longer prisoners of war. We hear the Americans are fifteen miles away in Wetzlar and will soon be here to set us free – meeting with only little opposition. Everyone naturally very excited. Americans are expected at any moment.

At 4.30 pm we were told that the Commandant realised that his responsibilities according to the Geneva Convention were to hand us over to Allied troops and therefore the guard had to be replaced and we were prisoners of war again! We are prevented from leaving the camp without an escort. We paraded again for our own benefit and, in case of trouble, we shall use the factory air raid shelters – otherwise we stay here. The guards have been replaced but are very friendly.

Plenty of traffic moving north; also much foot traffic, all showing white cloths. Very little air activity considering the closeness of the war. The Americans are reported near Giessen, five miles away. They <u>may</u> be here tomorrow! Rumours of a move are very strong! A German general arrived this evening at 7.30 pm asking for the Commandant. Fully expected to be moved but nothing happened till 11.45 pm when we were all asleep and the Senior British Officer came in to say that we were definitely not being moved BUT that this area was to be defended and more Flak was coming to reinforce that already here. So there it is. When the battle gets warm we shall go to the factory shelters!

<u>28th March 1945</u>

The camp naturally awoke in a state of great excitement at the possibility of being FREE today and I heard close gunfire at 6.00 am. After that we heard small-arms fire, then masses of refugees and prisoners of war and transport crowding the only road we can see. Noises grew louder and louder. At 10.00 am we had a trial run to the shelter to be ready for later. Gunfire increased in intensity till 2.45 pm when it became close enough for the order to be given that those who 'wished' could go to the shelter. Nearly all the camp went but I stayed on with a few others until 3.15 pm when the salvos³ came very close, whistling quite near us, and we were ordered to the shelter. There we met the rest of the camp and lived on the rumour coming from the rear party left at the huts.

At 3.40 pm we got a message in the shelter that the American guns had been <u>seen</u> and that the German troops were retreating west to east and south to north, up the River Lahn, and quite visible from the huts. Am writing this in the shelter. A message came in that at 17.10 pm our homemade Union Jack was hoisted at the camp by our rear party, and that forty armoured vehicles had passed after having sprayed the place pretty heavily with machine-gun fire; our party were in slit trenches with white flags but no one hurt. The Americans could not be bothered with white flags until they were certain no opposition was forthcoming.

At 17.30 pm today, Wednesday the 28th March, I left the shelter and saw all the American tanks, etc., lined up across the river – what a terrific thrill! Soon after, we left the shelters and returned to the camp FREE men! Some Americans came across and we knew that we had been relieved by CCA of the 7th Armoured Division of the 1st American Army.⁴ All our guard are now prisoners of war and we are delighted! We are also very, very grateful that the war passed over us with so little activity and it is hard to believe that one is actually FREE.

<u>29th March 1945</u>

Masses of American transport in the town. The bounds of the camp have been extended and we can go for good walks. Our only thoughts are for getting away from these horrible huts and stone floors and messy feeding arrangements – and incidentally, from the thousands of foreign workers who are also all crowding in on us. We realise it may take some time and we also realise that the war must be won before every other consideration. A German plane came over this evening and dropped two bombs near the station – no one hurt! An American division in Giessen and a brigade in Lollar.

We are now very organised by our own people and one naturally rather resents it. However, it keeps the brigadiers amused. We had a hot meal in the factory canteen this evening, quite a change from messing about with tins.

Life is really good these days anyway; liberated, nothing could have been finer. There were actually eleven Shermans[5] in the column, which made contact with us. No light in the huts of course, and now all the water has failed and it has to be brought in barrels; this really is a terrible place. Still we <u>are</u> free.

30th March 1945

Washed in the River Lahn this morning as there was no water at the camp. There are no bounds now and we can go where we like. Walked all through the village in the afternoon and then ran into the French Liaison Officer with the 3rd American Corps and went round the town with him. Returned to camp to find that we are being moved into billets in the town this evening.

We moved at 5.00 pm and I was allotted to a very nice little villa (Frau Siebaum, 10, Horst Wessel Street!); there were five of us there and I shared a room with Bertie MacLeay, as we have all been split up into nationalities and am therefore separated from Joe Johansen to my great regret.

It really was lovely being in a civilised house with nice furniture and a soft bed. We had a meal in the factory canteen where they provided as much wine as we could drink. We later returned to our little house where we had an omelette and some of our own coffee and went to bed very tired at about 11.30 pm I had my second typhus inoculation today, which has upset me a bit too. The feather bed was much too soft and I had a very rotten night: it will take some time to get used to civilisation again.

31st March 1945

Got up late but managed to 'acquire', from a German store I got to hear of, a German pack and water bottle – makes a very great difference – good condition too. After lunch we were warned of <u>another</u> move, this time very much for the WORSE as we are to leave our lovely little house. Lunch, incidentally, was a really magnificent rabbit stew! We are being moved to Dulag-Luft at Wetzlar.[6] Back to a camp, and huts and crowds of people, etc., etc.! We left Lollar in American transport at 3.00 pm and eventually arrived here about 3.45 pm and found everything just what one might expect – very crowded rooms, usual huts, communal feeding, over one thousand strong, etc., etc., all the horrors of prison life, the only difference being no Germans! We are only allowed out for two hours at a time and then only ten at a time and the town is out of bounds! Food is good but that's just about ALL!

1st April 1945

A rumour that we <u>may</u> leave for home on Thursday, in four days' time – let's hope it's true. To have allowed us a taste of civilisation and then bring us back to this is really too cruel for words. Easter Sunday! No water, no light, hard beds, etc. Still we can take it and we are FREE now – patience.

2nd April 1945
This morning at 7.10 am we were warned to move off at 8.45 am by lorry to leave from Giessen aerodrome for England! Terrific excitement and flap and throwing away of everything but the bare essentials. The order then added that as summer time came on last night the time was now 8.10 am and we therefore had little more than half an hour! Actually the American transport did not come for us till 11.45 am

In three quarters of an hour we were at Giessen aerodrome. The damage there is terrific. The weather was bad and we spent all day there till 6.50 pm when we were told that no planes were coming and that we all had to go back to Wetzlar. Very, very disappointing. Our rooms have all been swept clean of everything we left behind and here we are, back again where we started from!

Taken on return to England
for Military Pass, 3 April 1945.

Best Wishes for a Happy Return Home
from :-

AUSTRALIAN RED CROSS
BRITISH RED CROSS & ST. JOHN
CANADIAN RED CROSS
INDIAN RED CROSS & ST. JOHN AMBULANCE ASSOCIATION
JOINT COUNCIL OF ST. JOHN AND RED CROSS OF NEW ZEALAND
SOUTH AFRICAN RED CROSS

We Salute You and wish you the very
Best of Luck.

Found in Red Cross parcel given Casdagli on return.

20. MY CUP OF HAPPINESS

<u>3rd April 1945</u>

Again warned to be ready at 7.30 am! The weather was dark and overcast and it was raining. However the transport arrived early and we were soon off, but the roads were terribly slippery and the truck two ahead of me skidded right round, bruised several officers and split its back axle, ending up with its tailboard hard up against a bridge. It was sheer <u>bad</u> and reckless driving and a miracle that no one was hurt. The occupants piled into the other trucks and we arrived again at Giessen aerodrome at 8.30 am. The weather was shocking and we settled down to a long wait – and got it. It was not till 1.10 pm that we saw our first plane, a Dakota C-47,[1] and then they started coming over in streams.

The weather has cleared. They really are to take us to England.

At long last at 2.10 pm I had my seat with twenty-four others in a plane called 'Buck – i – Kid'!! We had three very nice young crew and talked to them very earnestly about getting us home safely! We said we wanted no tricks and quoted the mishap in the lorry! They saw our point!

At 2.10 pm we really took off and left Germany for GOOD! At 3.10 pm we were over Liege and I was promptly sick, but we had left Germany for good. We crossed the Rhine, south of Bonn and went over Aachen, we saw clearly the Siegfried Line defences[2] and the recent battlefields. Clear sunny weather.

At 4.30 pm we were actually over the Channel and at 4.40 pm. I saw the white cliffs of Dover, which we have dreamt of for so long. We flew over Canterbury and I was sick again, we skirted London but flew over Windsor, which we saw clearly and I looked down on my future home.[3]

We landed at a large aerodrome east of Oxford[4] at 5.45 pm where we were made very welcome by the RAF who took us to a hut for tea and cakes. There I spoke to my first female for almost five years, a little ATS who took my coat! We were too excited and dazed to know really what was happening, but we were made very welcome.

After tea, we had a really delightful run in a bus from the aerodrome to Reception Camp 90, at Chalfont St Giles – one and a quarter hours' run in the lovely April sunshine of the evening – arriving there at about 8.30 pm. The organisation was absolutely SPLENDID. I got some clean clothes, sent a telegram, drew ten pounds (sterling) and had an excellent supper in a very short time. Dog tired, I went to bed for a perfect night's sleep.

They saw our point! At 2.10 p.m. we really took off and left
Germany for GOOD! At 3.10 p.m. we were over Liege and I was
promptly sick, but we had left Germany for good. We crossed
the Rhine, South of Bonn and went over Aachen, we saw clearly
the Siegfried line defences and the recent battle fields -
clear sunny weather. At 4.30 p.m. we were actually over the
Channel and at 4.40 p.m. I saw the white cliffs of Dover, which
we have dreamt of for so long. We flew over Canterbury and I
was sick again, we skirted London but flew over Windsor which
we saw clearly and I looked down on my future home. We landed
at a large aerodrome east of Oxford at 5.45 p.m. where we were
made very welcome by the R.A.F. who took us to a hut for tea and
cakes. There I spoke to my first female for almost four years,
a little bit of an A.T.S. who took my coat! We were too excited and dazed to know really what was happening but we were made
very welcome. After tea we had a really delightful run in a bus
from the aerodrome to Reception Camp Ninety, at Chalfont St. Giles
- one and a quarter hours run in the lovely April sunshine of the
evening, arriving there at about 8.30 p.m. The organisation was
absolutely SPLENDID - I got some clean clothes, sent a telegram,
drew ten pounds (sterling) and had an excellent supper in a very
short time - dog tired I went to bed for a perfect nights sleep.

4th

Got up early to complete the formalities and again we were
pushed through at terrific speed - Xrayed for T.B., dental and
medical inspection, given leave warrants, food cards, clothing
coupons, etc., and actually finished the whole job by 9.45 a.m!
The Colonel of the camp sent me to the bus stop in his car where
I caught the 10 a.m. bus for Windsor - I was in an absolute dazel
Arrived at Windsor and took another bus for Oakley Green and
arrived at High Trees at 11.20 a.m. Joyce had gone to Ludgrove
to meet Tony and bring him home for the holidays! I went down
the drive and waited for them at the gate at 12 noon they arrived
and my cup of happiness was FULL. Since 25th September, 1939 I
had not seen them. I am on forty-two days leave with only the
prospect of a medical board to worry me. And so writing these
last words in my own home among my own people I now close this
journal and Thank God for my safe return.

THE END

75

Last page of typed diary.

<u>4th April 1945</u>

Got up early to complete the formalities and again we were pushed through at terrific speed – X-rayed for TB, dental and medical inspection, given leave warrants, food cards, clothing coupons, etc., and actually finished the whole job by 9.45 am! The Colonel of the camp sent me to the bus stop in his car where I caught the 10.00 am bus for Windsor – I was in an absolute daze!

Arrived at Windsor and took another bus for Oakley Green and arrived at High Trees at 11.20 am. Joyce had gone to Ludgrove[5] to meet Tony and bring him home for the holidays! I went down the drive and waited for them at the gate. At 12 noon they arrived and my cup of happiness was FULL. I had not seen them since 25th September 1939.

I am on forty-two days leave with only the prospect of a medical board to worry me. And so, writing these last words in my own home among my own people, I now close this journal and thank God for my safe return.

THE END

EPILOGUE

Casdagli wrote 'THE END' after the final entry of his diary, but it wasn't the end – at least, not the happy end Casdagli supposed.

The entry states he arrived at High Trees at 11.20 am on Thursday, 4 April 1945. The War Office hadn't been able to notify Joyce of her husband's return due to 'prevailing circumstances'; and when, on 9 April, they did, they sent the card to an address where Joyce no longer lived.

As luck would have it, Casdagli, one of the first POWs to be repatriated after liberation, wanted his homecoming to be a surprise. He sent a telegram to his mother in Cairo with the news but he didn't telephone or cable Joyce to let her know he was back.

When he walked up the drive and was told at the house Joyce had gone to Ludgrove School to bring Tony home for the Easter holidays, it was his turn to be surprised. Easter was over and school would have broken up for the holidays at least a week before.

He walked back down the drive to wait for his wife and son. The school was only twelve miles away. They wouldn't be long and, sure enough, at noon, they arrived. After being re-united, they drove up to the house. There, Casdagli was put into a guest bedroom where he later spent the night alone.

Early next morning, Casdagli caught a train to London and went straight to the War Office to ask for an overseas posting. Rightly or wrongly, he believed another had taken his place in his wife's affections. Divorce proceedings were started on the grounds of his alleged adultery. He did not contest the case.

In those early days of repatriation, Casdagli kept some promises he'd made in prison. He had vowed however hungry he was, he wouldn't eat the contents of his emergency ration tin until he was back in England. He kept that promise and the tin, which became one of his most treasured possessions. Next, he sent Rolex a cheque for the watch they'd sent him in Oflag IX-A/H three years earlier. Rolex replied saying they were delighted he'd survived. Lastly, he went to a Lyons Corner House and ordered a dish of whipped cream, something he'd been dreaming of for years. Lyons Corner Houses were popular, inexpensive restaurants in London where people could eat, have a drink, listen to the band and dance in grand surroundings. When the cream came, Casdagli couldn't eat it. It was too rich and, in his words, he was 'blubbing too much'.

April found him back in Windsor where, according to an unknown local newspaper, on 25 April 1945, Casdagli gave 'a very interesting account of his experiences' to the monthly meeting of the Windsor and District Association

Shaftesbury Hospital 1945. Detail. 210 x 195 mm

Silver Dunhill lighter, 1945.

of Relatives of Prisoners of War. It was, states the report, 'of special interest, as many members had heard news of the release of their relatives by the victorious allied armies. Some had already arrived home and were present, including Lt Col. Everitt from Oflag 79, near Brunswick, and Lt Wheeler.'

On 8 May 1945, the Second World War ended in Europe.

That summer, Casdagli was admitted to Shaftesbury Military Hospital for the hernia operation he'd been advised to have over four years before. During his stay there, he embroidered a shoulder bag with the hospital's name and the year in its design.

On 6 August 1945, the United States dropped an atomic bomb on Hiroshima and three days later, dropped a second on Nagasaki. Over 100,000 people were killed on impact. Many thousands more died later.

On 2 September 1945, Japan formally surrendered and the Second World War was finally over.

Casdagli described what happened next in his life in a letter to Dilys Powell, the film critic and author, dated 27 January 1974:

'Whilst in hospital, I learned that a British Military Mission to Greece, based in Athens, was being formed. As, for personal reasons, I wanted to get out of England as soon as I could, I volunteered and, being able to speak Greek, I was accepted, and the autumn of 1945 found me back again in Greece.'

Athens was reeling from the Occupation and civil war. Menda had fled to safety in England with Alexis, now five, and her husband was in Egypt. Casdagli knew no one. However, a British woman there, Dolly Kiokpas, married to a Greek dentist, held open house on Sundays. No stranger to suffering herself, having lived through the Occupation in Athens, she took Casdagli under her wing. He regained his fitness and became the Athens Squash Rackets Champion, 1945. His prize was a silver Dunhill lighter.

Later that year, Captain A. V. Chivers joined the Mission. His arrival prompted Casdagli to fulfil another pledge made in prison, which was to write to Chivers, makers of jelly and jams, concerning their jellies. Captain Chivers duly provided the address and, on 21 January 1946, Casdagli wrote to the Manager of Chivers as follows:

'Dear Sir,

I cannot give you the exact date on which it was discovered that your jelly cubes, which came to us in Red Cross parcels, had the properties of duplicating gelatine if properly treated. I personally saw maps printed off your cubes in 1941.

I did not myself become intimately connected with the printing business

Rubber stamp impressions, some made with the aid
of Chivers jelly cubes. '*Geprüft*' means 'passed'.

until April 1944 when, in the company of Major Deighton RA and Captain Hutchinson NZEF, I formed part of the official Mapping and Printing Team at Oflag XII-B. This was a senior officers' camp and included Maj. Gen. Sir Victor Fortune. The escaping and mapping etc. came directly under Brigadier R. L. Taverner.

Our problem was to produce as many maps of the area around our camp on as a large a scale as possible in the shortest time. This policy was adopted for several reasons, the three main ones being: the possibility of one day being left by our German guards on the approach of Allied troops and hence the necessity of knowing our exact whereabouts; secondly, the possibility that there might be fighting in our area and the need for knowing the position of Allied troops; and thirdly, normal routine escaping plans.

We also undertook the printing of forged identity cards and passes and German censor stamps. I can safely say any diaries or papers which officers in our camp did not wish the Germans to examine too closely were 'censored' by us!

That gives you roughly the background and the need for a duplicating process. Now for the practical side.

Whenever Chivers Jellies arrived in Red Cross parcels (which was all too seldom – printing was sometimes held up on this account), they were removed from our 'tin store' by the British officer in charge of the cookhouse and handed to the escaping committee. Naturally, the crystals were of no use to us and the gelatine cubes only could be used.

The procedure was to melt down the cubes from three or preferably four packets in a tin without the addition of any water then pour off the liquid into a specially manipulated tray and allow to set hard. When the gelatine had set, it was necessary to wash the surface with warm water to remove the sugar which comes to the top and renders the surface sticky. Before this was discovered, many hours of work were wasted by maps being torn through having stuck to the jelly. Incidentally we found that the lemon jellies reacted much better than raspberry or other flavours!!

We produced our copying ink by powdering down the lead from copying pencils, adding water and then boiling the liquid to make it as concentrated as possible. The master copy of the map to be printed was traced with the ink on to very thin strong paper (the best we ever had was the wrapping of some religious pamphlets sent to our camp from Switzerland). The master copy completed, the next and by far the most difficult operation was to roll it out on the jelly without smudging it. Trial and error eventually proved that the best way was to roll the master copy on to a pencil, place the pencil at one end of the tray and, with an even pressure, unroll the map on to the surface of the jelly. After this, all was plain sailing.

Wendy Casdagli, née Nicholson.

British Consulate, Volos,
January, 1945.

Gold Cross of the Royal
Order of the Phoenix.

It was not necessary to leave the master copy down for more than a minute before peeling it off. A perfect impression was then left on the jelly and under good conditions and, if the weather was not too hot, twenty-five serviceable maps could be produced from one master copy – on occasions as many as thirty were obtained.

Naturally, the greatest care had to be taken to prevent any German from observing our movements and literally hundreds of man-hours were spent on these operations and on 'stooging', in other words, being on guard at certain points to give warning of approaching Huns.

We often used to say that when we were finally liberated and at home again we would write to Chivers and tell them to what use their jelly cubes were put and of what inestimable value they were to us in this particular work.

This letter is entirely unofficial but I thought it might interest you to know of our activities in prison as far as your firm were concerned. We often wondered if you had any suspicions that your jelly cubes were being put to this use. Since our liberation last April, my colleagues and I have become separated and I very much doubt if the others have written to you.

I hope you will excuse this rather long rambling letter – it all seems rather childish now but at the time it was of vital importance to us and certainly the maps we produced were most wanted.

I remain yours sincerely,

A. T. Casdagli,

ex-POW, no. 3311, Crete, 1941-1945'

One Sunday, Dolly introduced Casdagli to a beautiful spy with flaming red hair, Wendy Nicholson, a Captain in the Special Operations Executive (SOE). Casdagli was smitten and he soon became her 'beloved Cas'.

In Athens, Casdagli met Mercy Money-Coutts, the archaeologist. Knowing he wanted to stay on in Greece after his one year's appointment to the BMM ended, she asked if he would be interested in being in Crete as the Curator of the Villa Ariadne at the Minoan Palace of Knossos. Casdagli, in his letter to Dilys Powell, whose book, *The Villa Ariadne*, he'd just read, takes over the story,

'Naturally, I wholeheartedly agreed that my name should go forward. She had warned me that the job had always been given to an archaeologist, but there was a scheme afoot to appoint a Greek speaking business man, used to agriculture, and used to managing men, who could administer not only the Villa but also the agricultural lands and vines which belonged to it.

'However, having got as far as a 'short list', she eventually showed me a letter signed by Sir John Myers saying that it had been decided to appoint an

With Alexis Penny, Volos 1948.

HMS Euryalus.

Christening, Alexis Penny,
19 September 1949.

archaeologist as usual, and as you explain in *The Villa Ariadne*, Mr Hutchinson was re-appointed. Within a month, however, I had been offered and accepted the post of British Consul in Volos. So my plans to stay in Greece succeeded in this unexpected way. Little did I know the Foreign Office were opening the post in anticipation of the second round of the Greek Civil War!'

In January 1947, Casdagli took up his post in Volos and, indeed, found himself 'in the thick' of the Civil War. Wendy joined him there and they married on 23 September. They lived in an apartment overlooking the port of Volos, flanked by mountains in which bitter fighting was taking place between communist and nationalist factions. Causalities were heavy. More people died in the Civil War in Greece than in the Occupation.

In November, Wendy became pregnant.

In early 1948, Joyce married Frank Hargrove, Casdagli's friend, solicitor and fellow Old Harrovian and Grovite, to whom he had given his Power of Attorney in 1943 from prison.

That spring, an uncharacteristic muddle of Casdagli's making came to light, about being Mentioned in Dispatches. On 19 April 1948, he writes to his mother.

'Many thanks for sending me on the card from the War Office – it was of course quite alright to open it. I am afraid that I missed the point for quite a long time! I thought it was to advise me about the first mention, the certificate for which I already have; but that was in the London Gazette of 1941. This new Mention is a second one published in the Gazette of 1945, and therefore probably not unconnected with the MI9 work I was doing for the War Office while inside. I had expected (conceitedly???) some sort of "thank you" and I presume this must be it.'

This honour was followed in July by another. On 10 August, again writing to his mother, he tells her,

'As a matter of fact I have a bit of news for you all! His Majesty the King of the Hellenes (you know, the Paul person, who wants to take Cyprus off us) has seen fit to decorate me with the Gold Cross of the Royal Order of the Phoenix! I have had information from the War Office that they hold the insignia and diploma, and that permission has been obtained from King George VI (whom the Lord preserve) for me to accept and wear the decoration. I know nothing else except that. I don't know if it is an order which has different classes; if so, they do not tell me what class I have been given. I suppose you will all wonder what it is for? It is certainly nothing to do with the Consular work here, because the information comes from the War Office and not the Foreign Office. I presume that it dates back to my imprisonment with General Kaffatos. He told me he had recommended General Fortune

At the factory gates.

'Injection moulded' Perspex keys rings
made by Williaam J. Cox.

Kersal Hill, Wigginton, Tring, 1962.

Playing squash with his nephew, Alexis Lykiard,
Tring, October 1956.

and myself for a Greek decoration for our help etc. to Greek prisoners in Crete and Germany. I can only presume that it is that recommendation which has, at long last, found the light of day. It might, of course, have something to do with my time at the BMM but I do NOT think so. So now you know just as much about it as I do! It sounds very grand, but it is probably very small beer; however, I am secretly very bucked about it! '

Two days later, Wendy was roped into an army helicopter and flown to the Military Hospital in Phaleron, near Athens, where she was safely delivered of a daughter. Which is where I come in.

The following year, on 19 September 1949, I was christened with water from the upturned bell of the British destroyer, HMS Euryalus, in the port of Volos. Legally, the ship was British 'soil' which meant my parents could get a British passport for me in case an emergency exit from this war-torn zone was necessary. Dolly Kiokpas was one of my godparents.

In 1950, after his three years of service, Casdagli's post in Volos was 'closed'. We returned to England where, in July, my father had another operation, this time at the Stretford Memorial Hospital in Manchester. Casdagli re-joined Emmanuel Casdagli & Sons in Manchester, but the war had knocked the heart out of the business. It could not compete with cheaper imports of cloth from Japan and Italy.

In 1952, Casdagli went into partnership with his youngest brother, Theo, who had set up Williaam [sic] J. Cox., a successful plastics moulding company in Tring, a small town in Hertfordshire in the south of England. Theo ran the office in London and Casdagli ran the factory in Tring. In the early 1950s, Perspex was a new and exciting material. Williaam J. Cox made many things, including roof lights, the nose of fighter planes, revolutionary incubators for premature or sick babies as well as the barrels of Parker Pens and commercial signage.

Tring had two squash courts, built by Casdagli's Old Harrovian friend, Victor Rothschild. Squash courts were very unusual in those days. Casdagli played a lot. He was the captain of the Tring Squash Team, played for the county and for the Jesters, a worldwide organization of over 3,000 elected members, mostly squash players. He was virtually unbeatable. He stopped playing, at Wendy's request, when he was fifty-six.

Casdagli was also embroidering again, predominantly geometric patterns based on traditional Greek designs. He was making table-clothes, double bedspreads, even small carpets and tapestry for chairs and stools. He embroidered virtually every day for at least three hours until he was 87.

During these Tring years, he went to Crete at least twice to stay with General Kaffatos in his village, Skines, near Chania. These visits to 'his

Swallowtail 1954. 620 x 480 mm

Geometric embroidery 1981. 500 x 500 mm

General' meant a lot to him. Kaffatos died in 1958, aged 70.

On 10 April that year, Casdagli's birthday, his mother also died, aged 86.

In December, 1958, a parcel arrived for Casdagli from Germany, addressed to the offices of Emmanuel Casdagli & Sons in Manchester, which were now closed. Inside was the portrait the Earl Haig painted of Casdagli in Oflag XII-B, Hadamar, in 1944, which he'd had to abandon on liberation by the Americans! A fishmonger in Frankfurt, Carl Gessen, had found it in an attic and decided to return it to the hastily scribbled address on the back. It had been forwarded by Neild, Son and Lees, a Manchester chartered acountants, who were given Casdagli's business address by a Mr Potts. Haig, now a full-time artist living in Scotland, was told of the portrait's reappearance and was delighted. Casdagli sent it to him for him to sign, something he hadn't done in Germany.

Casdagli had never lost touch with Al Kenny, 'the Salford Dreadnought', who taught him boxing in the holidays when a schoolboy at Harrow. Several times, Kenny, as my father called him, and his wife came down from Manchester to stay with us in Tring. One on these visits, Kenny gave my father a recent photograph of himself, on which he'd written 'To A. T. Casdagli, an apt and able pupil and great friend, from his Pal, Al Kenny, February 1961.'

In 1962, Casdagli built a house in the village of Wigginton, near Tring, designed by the architect, Edward Samuel, and called it Kersal Hill, after the family house in Salford.

That year, for the first time since 1950, we went back to Greece for a holiday on the island of Myconos. Myconos was beautiful, very quiet, and had, at this time, just two cars and one tarmac road. Walking along the beach one day, Casdagli happened to meet a cousin of his, Paul Gripari, who he hadn't seen for years. Paul asked him if he'd like to buy his garden which overlooked Myconos' harbour. Casdagli agreed and plans were soon drawn up for a small house there.

On 9 May 1963, Casdagli's sister, Menda was suddenly taken ill and died in the Royal Victoria Hospital, Boscombe three days later of infective hepatitis. She was 53.

In 1964, the house on Myconos was finished. Casdagli called that house Kersal Hill as well.

In June 1965, Frank Hargrove died, aged 64.

On 31 July 1965, Casdagli retired from the factory. There was a big party and he was given a Rolex watch and a card signed by everyone. He was overwhelmed. He took out the clean white handkerchief he always kept in his pocket and sobbed into it. No one knew what to do. Finally, he managed to say, remembering Lyons Corner House,

Menda Lykiard,
1910 – 1963.

Second Rolex watch, 31 July 1965.

Kersal Hill, top centre, with tree, right of the mast,
Myconos Harbour, 1964.

'I haven't blubbed like this since I left prison.'

'Don't worry, Cas,' called out Keith Mitchener who'd worked with him for years, 'you'll be back there soon!'

'That's just what I needed to get me back on my feet!' he said, drying his eyes and putting the handkerchief back in his pocket. Then the party really got into full swing.

In 1967, Casdagli and Wendy sold Kersal Hill in Wigginton and moved to London. They then divided their time between their flat in Highgate Village, and Kersal Hill in Myconos. Two years later, they decided to live in Athens and Myconos full time, only coming back to England for a month or two a year. This arrangement lasted for almost ten years until they sold Kersal Hill in Myconos and re-domiciled in England again.

In June 1978, Joyce, Casdagli's first wife, died, aged 72.

After her death, Casdagli transcribed his diary and, in 1982, gave the typescript and some other documents to the Archives of the Imperial War Museum (IWM). These included his letters to Joyce for the period 17 March 1944 to 18 January 1945, many of which have coded messages in them. Two are from a fictional nephew, 'John Simpson', also containing coded information. Casdagli explains more in a letter to Mr Reed of the Imperial War Museum (IWM), dated 8 September 1982:

'About coding. I have always been scared of talking about this too much, because of the Official Secrets Act, but I now realise that there cannot be many restrictions after a gap of 40 years! After the war, I heard from my wife, now dead, what happened her end. Apparently, an officer, obviously from MI9, called on her and told her that some of my letters would contain information for him and that therefore all my mail would go to the War Office first. There, the coded messages were marked with red ticks, deciphered and the letters returned to her. And she was not too worry if some of my letters sounded rather stilted and not quite natural. In fact, it was rather hard to encode messages without making some of the sentences rather odd.

'After I had been home some time, I had a call from Beaconsfield, where MI9 had their set-up, and they asked me if I would like to see over the UK end of the business. When there, I was asked if I would like to meet my 'nephew'. I said, "You mean John Simpson?" They said, "Yes", and then wheeled in a WAAF, about 4 foot high!' A WAAF is a member of the Women's Auxiliary Air Force.

In 1983, Tony, who married twice and has five children, was made a CBE in the New Year's Honour List. In 1984, he retired as a Captain in the Royal Navy. Casdagli was extremely proud.

Casdagli was also thrilled, when in 1988, Dr David Rolf quoted from his

Casdagli arriving in Crete, 23 November 1940.
Courtesy of the Imperial War Museum and British Council.

Casdagli, detail.

diary several times in his book, *Prisoners of the Reich*, (Leo Cooper). The diary is quoted again in 2004 in *The Colditz Myth* by S. P. MacKenzie, (Oxford University Press). Casdagli is also mentioned twice in Myles Hildyard's *It is Bliss Here*, (Bloomsbury Publishing).

In September 1987, Casdagli and Wendy celebrated their fortieth wedding anniversary. They loved each other as deeply as ever.

On 14 November of that year, Jack Hamson, Casdagli's dear friend from Crete and fellow POW, died. Their paths hadn't crossed much since the end of the war. Jack had gone back to Trinity College, Cambridge, become a professor and had an illustrious academic career, including being elected a Bencher and then Treasurer to the Honourable Society of Gray's Inn, in London, one of the four professional associations for barristers and judges. He also became a QC, (Queen's Council), a mark of outstanding ability.

Jack did write a book about his war experiences but not 'A Day in the Life of a Don', as he'd joked in Oflag X-C, Lübeck. *Liber in Vinculis or The Mock Turtle's Adventure* is an intense meditation on his actions and the events leading up to his capture in which he finds the sense of loveliness and horror go hand in hand. As Jack and Casdagli were in the same room in the same prison for several months, it must surely be possible that while Jack was writing his book, Casdagli was writing this diary. In 1989, after his death, as was his wish, *Liber in Vinculis* was published by Trinity College, Cambridge.

In 1991, for the fiftieth anniversary of the Battle of Crete, the Greek Government invited all Allied Veterans of the Battle to the island to take part in two weeks of commemorations, exhibitions and feasts to celebrate of the courage of the Veterans and the Cretan people. The first week of the programme was in Heraklion in the east of the island. I joined my parents for the second week in Chania in the west.

One afternoon, while my mother was resting, my father and I walked down to the harbour to see an exhibition of photographs of the Battle of Crete in the Venetian Arsenal.

We went through narrow entrance to the exhibition in the huge vaults of the arsenal where an enormous photograph was suspended by chains from the roof. It was, perhaps inevitably, the photograph which begins this diary: of a British troop ship arriving in Crete in 1940; only one soldier on the deck of the warship is looking at the camera, Casdagli. I stared at it and said,

'Dad! It's you!'

Casdagli, fifty years on, stopped and looked up at himself. People around us stopped too. Some exclaimed. Some crossed themselves. Someone fetched the curator who happened to be there. She looked at Dad and then at the photo and then she exclaimed too! The only person who did not appear surprised

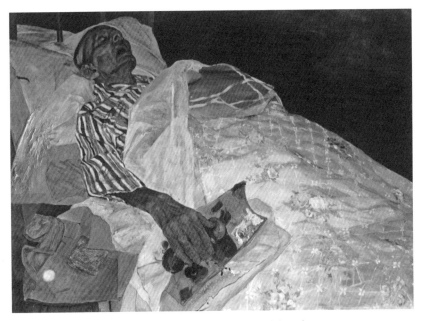

The Last Time I Saw My Beautiful Father.
Alexis Penny Casdagli, 2006, oil on canvas. 122 x 91 mm

While there is life there is happiness. 320 x 565 mm

was my father. The curator arranged for the British Council to send Casdagli a copy of the photograph. The accompanying letter from the Council's Tom Pickett said, 'Recognising yourself in the main picture of such an exhibition must have been a pleasant surprise and quite a strange experience for you...I hope you have recovered from the shock!'

Towards the end of his life, when Casdagli was in the nursing home adjoining the flats where Wendy lived, and didn't know quite who anyone was, I sometimes sat up with him at nights, reading or drawing. Once, when he looked at me quizzically, I asked him,

'Do you know who I am, Dad?'

'Whoever you are, lady,' he said, 'don't leave me.'

And I don't believe I have.

On 1 December 1996, a nurse, who was very fond of him, came into his room to give him a little lunch.

'Do you like apricots, Mr Cas?' she asked him.

'Rather,' he replied and had a sip or two of syrup. She stayed with him and was with him at 5 pm when he died, aged 90.

Wendy was exceptionally brave. In the spring of 1997, we scattered Casdagli's ashes in Crete in the wide valley overlooked by the Palace of Knossos from the footpath of the Villa Ariadne. In spite of being in a lot of physical pain and missing him like mad, Wendy decided to get a kick out of her 'golden years' and she enjoyed the time she had left. She died on 17th January 1999. I scattered her ashes into that same wide valley in Crete and if there is an afterlife – which my father was adamant there was not – he was there waiting for her. She is still very much missed. They both are.

In 1984, aged 78, Casdagli made another embroidery with a swallowtail. He put a quote in it from Tolstoi's *War and Peace*, which he read in captivity between 5th and 9th November, 1944. It was: 'While there is life there is happiness'. With Wendy's encouragement, he entered it for a competition and it won him runner-up to the *Needlewoman of the Year 1984*. He was tickled pink! His prize was a circular sewing box in which he kept his silks, needles and scissors for the rest of his life.

THE END

MAP
ENDNOTES
BIBLIOGRAPHY
ABBREVIATIONS
INDEX

Map of Prisoner of War Camps, 1944

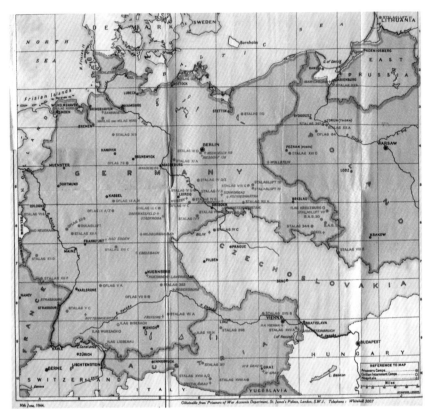

Casdagli's Red Cross map.

ENDNOTES

Capture
1. Last Days of Freedom

1 The Battle of Crete began on the morning of Friday 20 May 1941 when the Germans launched their airbourne invasion of the island in wave after wave of paratroop drops in an operation code named Operation Mercury. The battle lasted twelve days. Crete was of great strategic importance. The harbour at Suda Bay was the largest in the Mediterranean Sea, ideal for naval operations and the island could be used as a base for troops heading to the Northern African theatre of war. Due to a series of strategic mistakes made by their commanders, the Allies snatched 'defeat out of the jaws of victory'. The troops on the ground put up a fierce defence, aided by the unparalled bravery of the civilian population

2 The H(is) M(ajesty's) A(ustralian) S(hip) Sydney was sunk almost a year later on 19 November 1941 off the Western Australian coast after being ambushed by a German ship with the loss of its entire crew of 645. The wreck's location was Australia's biggest naval mystery until it was discovered 67 years later on 17 March 2008 about 93 miles off Shark Bay.

3 'Οχι' means 'no' in Greek. At dawn on 28 October 1940, the Italian dictator, Benito Mussolini, sent an ultimatum to Ioannis Metaxas, the Greek Prime Minister, demanding that Greece allow Axis forces, massed in Albania, to occupy 'strategic areas' in Greece or face war. At 5.30 am, Metaxas said 'no' and Greece entered the Second World War. Since 1942, 'Oxi Day' has been celebrated in Greece to commemorate that brave refusal.

4 An intensive or sudden attack or bombing coming from the air.

5 At 8:00 am on 20 May 1941, hundreds of German paratroopers were dropped along the northern coast of Crete in the start of an airborne invasion of the island. They fell in compact groups at the rate of one man per second from Ju-52s, (Junkers transport planes), guns having already been parachuted down ahead of them. Whilst in the air – only seven seconds – they carried pistols. Casualties were heavy; for example, within the first six hours of the invasion, one company of the III Battalion, 1st Assault Regiment, lost 112 of its 126 paratroopers and by the end of the day, 400 of the battalion's 600 men had been killed.

6 King George II of Greece, an ardent anglophile, and his party had been hiding in the village of Perivolia but the Germans learnt of their whereabouts.

When the royal party were alerted to this, they fled to the hills and hid in a villa in Theriso. It was there that the prisoners who had been released earlier that day banged on the villa's doors, looking for food and weapons, unaware that the King of Greece, also fugitive, was within. Whatever anti-royalist sentiments they might have had, the prisoners did not betray the King, and continued their search elsewhere.

7   The King and his entourage were evacuated from Crete to Alexandria in Egypt by HMS Decoy on 22 May 1941.

8   A member of a clandestine subversive organisation working within a country to further an invading enemy's military and political aims.

9   Tinned boiled meat, usually beef, in white fat.

10 A very small sum in the Greek currency of the time.

11 Capt. R. F. Moody writes in the anthology Detour (London, Falcon Press, 1946): 'I saw the whole battalion make their bayonet charge on the Maleme aerodrome. The charge was proceeded by a "Haka" and was led by their Colonel.' A haka is a Maori war dance and their Colonel would have been a rangitira, or chieftain, among the Maori people.

12 Lt Sandbach, in Detour, describes the scene as follows: 'Dawn broke swiftly in a flawless sky on the morning of 1st June. No ripple disturbed the blue of the sea and the hill was quiet in the fresh morning air. The day was perfect but there was confusion and weariness amongst the men who thronged the narrow Sphakia valley. The news that the Navy could not return had come as a physical shock for them. Their actions became mechanical. Many settled down to destroy their weapons and equipment; some started to forage for food and water while others started the pitiful job of displaying white flags. Soon the length of the valley where the remnants of the Creforce had collected was draped with white tokens of surrender.'

13 A leading make of binoculars still sold.

14 The gold ring was engraved with the family crest of the Colossus of Rhodes, which was also the trade mark of Emmanuel Casdagli & Sons. It had 'χαλεπά τα καλά' as its motto, meaning 'good things have to be worked for.'

15 An antiseptic liquid disinfectant which is still sold today.

2. First Days of Captivity

1   Ju-52s, made by Junkers, were planes predominantly used for transporting troops although they also served as bombers and for dropping paratroops. Because the planes were slow and lightly armed against fighter bombers, they suffered terrible losses, as they did over Crete.

2   The Bralos Pass rises to an altitude of 1,475 feet above sea level.

3. A Real Nightmare

1   Salonika, or Thessaloniki, is the second largest city in Greece and an important commercial port. For centuries, the majority of its population were Jewish. On 8 April 1941, two days after the German invasion of Greece, it became the first major city to fall to the occupying forces. By June of that year, the pillaging and destruction of the city's infrastructure was well underway together with the merciless decimation of the city's starving population. In 1943, 60,000 Jews, virtually the city's entire Jewish population, were deported to concentration camps where almost all died.

2   The vast site of the Pavlos Melas Barracks stretched over an area of 380 acres. Built around 1906 during the Ottoman period, the Barracks were a death and torture camp as well as a prison and were to become one of Greece's main concentration camps, of which there were at least eight. Well over 1,750 'undesirables', patriots, Soviet, Polish and political prisoners, Roma, homosexuals, people with disabilities, intellectuals and common criminals, were executed there from 1941 to 1945. Capt. K.E. Herman in 'Salonika' in Detour, remembers being held there in July 1941 '...the name brings a numbness to the mind; just a space in time from which nothing stands out. A barrack square; blazing heat; derelict barracks; rear-seats in a cloud of flies; arrivals choking with ammonia fumes...'

3   Capt. K. E. Herman, again in Detour, writes: 'An Australian tried sleeping inside the barrack building; he came out half an hour later and counted seventy-three bed-bug bites on him. He was swollen up beyond recognition.'

4   The Red Cross played, and continues to play, a vital humanitarian role in relieving the suffering of people in crisis, whether due to conflict, poverty, disease or natural disaster. During the Second World War, the International Committee of the Red Cross (ICRC) worked tirelessly on behalf of prisoners of war (POWs), including the establishment of a Central Prisoner of War Agency with 40 million index cards; the conducting of 11,000 visits to POW camps; and the distribution of 450,000 tons of relief items and efforts to help

POWs and their loved ones to keep in touch.

5   W. J. Burton, in "Prisoners' Journey", in *Detour*, also describes this incident: 'One morning after a night of shots, shouts and terrified screams, five bullet-ridden Arabs littered the compound and were left for twelve hours as an example to anyone who contemplated escape.' *'Pour encourager les autres'* is French for 'to encourage the others' but is often used ironically, as it is here, about an action, such as a killing, which has been carried out as an example or warning to others to do what they have been told to do.

6   Three pounds and twelve shillings, or £3.60, (equivalent to £150 in 2012 value). The money was a loan and was re-paid to Germany out of wages POWs received in their home country.

7   In his piece 'Four July Suns' for the anthology *Backwater: Oflag IX A/H Lower Camp* (London, Frederick Muller, 1944), Esmond Lynn-Allen writes of what lectures meant in the life of a POW: 'As books or cards were very scarce, the bulk of the community spent its time in organising, delivering, or attending lectures...In the course of a single day, carrying one's wooden stool from corner to corner of the courtyards, one might listen to a talk by an accountant, a farmer, a barrister, an architect, or the skipper of a trawler.'

4. Cattle Truck Journey

1   This small magnifying glass in a brass frame is held to the eye to count threads in fabric to determine the weight of the cloth. Somehow, it was returned after being confiscated. Of sentimental value as it belonged to Emmanuel Casdagli, the founder of Emmanuel Casdagli & Sons, it was taken into war for good luck.

2   It was from Salonika station that practically the entire Jewish population of the city, having been herded into the Pavlos Melas Barracks, were transported by cattle trucks to the death camps of Auschwitz and Birkenau where almost all were killed.

3   Meat and vegetables.

4   The direct distance between Salonkia and Lübeck is about 1,400 miles but this journey took a circuitous route. At Marburg, the route doubled back on itself by going south, not north, to Landshut. At Leipzig it went east to Luckenwalde and then west to Hamburg and then on to Lübeck, making it a journey of over 2,000 miles.

5   Adolf Hitler, the *Führer* or Leader of Nazi Party, hated Lübeck. In 1932, it refused to let him campaign there; so, as punishment, in 1937, he ended its 700 years of independence and incorporated it into Hamburg.

6   An Oflag, from '*Offizierslager*', was a POW camp for officers. Stalags were camps for non-commissioned officers and other ranks while Stalag Lufts were for flying personnel, both commissioned and non-commissioned. These camps were for POWs, not civilians. Camps were identified by Roman numerals according to their military district and by letters for the individual camps in that district.

Oflag X-C, Lübeck
5. Prisoner 3311

1   In fact, Oflag X-C was a former German army camp. It had been converted into a POW camp with high barbed-wire fences, watchtowers with armed guards and Alsatian dogs roaming freely, especially at night.

2   In the event of death, this metal tag was snapped in two. One half was kept by the Germans and the other half sent to the deceased's family with his few remaining possessions. However, the tag was very useful as its width was one fifth of a German loaf but a German loaf was five widths of a tag plus one gram. Using the tag as a measure, each loaf could be divided into five with a raffle for the portion with the extra gram.

3   General Solon Kaffatos was the Senior Greek Officer in Crete and in charge of Military Personnel for the Greek Ministry of War. He was also a distinguished veteran of the First World War.

4   The General (or Special) List includes commissioned officers of the British Army who are members of the General Service Corps (GSC). The GSC, normally only active in wartime, is a holding unit for specialists and reservists not badged to any other regiment or corps.

5   Jack Hamson was also captured in Crete. He was a don at Trinity College Cambridge before being commissioned into the army in 1940. Fluent in Greek, he was detached to the Special Operations Executive (SOE) and sent to Crete to plan clandestine operations and resistance in the event of a German invasion. He was based in the Suda Bay area where he and met Casdagli and they became great friends.

6   Lübeck was the first German city attacked in substantial numbers by the RAF.

7 Any sort of space where prisoners made football or cricket pitches was invariably bounded on one side by a trip wire. The result was that the ball repeatedly went into the no-man's land between the trip wire and the main fence round the camp. A guard would ignore the prisoner fetching a ball from this 'dead' ground four or five times but the sixth time he would fire.

8 Allied POWs were protected by The Convention Relative to the Treatment of Prisoners of War, otherwise known as the Third Geneva Convention of 1929, to which Germany was also a signatory. The Geneva Convention recognises that military POWs have a duty to try to escape at all times and to aid others to that end; it forbids reprisals against those who are caught and limits punishment.

9 An orderly is a non-commissioned solider assigned to attend and perform various tasks for a commissioned officer who pays his wages himself.

10 The Geneva Convention, amongst other requirements, required Allied POWs to be lodged in the same conditions as German troops with adequately heated and lighted buildings and to eat comparable food. However, the Germans frequently made little attempt to keep the Convention and often openly despised it.

11 Group Captain Douglas Bader, the legless fighter pilot ace, who was immortalised in Paul Brickhill's book *Reach for the Sky* and a film of the same name, was also incarcerated in Oflag X-C at this time. He later wrote in articles for the *North American Newspaper Alliance*, 1945, that Commandant Glaesche, 'was an unpleasant gentleman who said that he had not got any copies of the Geneva Convention, which he did not know anything about anyhow.' Bader always maintained: 'Lübeck was the worst prison camp I came across in Germany.'

12 A hernia is a protrusion by tissue or organs through a wall or membrane which should contain it. Besides the bulge, symptoms include pain and a heavy or dragging sensation in the groin.

13 Bader writes of this incident in his articles for *North American Newspaper Alliance*, 1945: 'A British bomber in trouble unloaded a basket of incendiaries on the German officers' mess, outside the camp. This was very satisfying to the prisoners, since it destroyed the mess.' (A 'mess' is a place where its members eat and socialise.) Dr Rubli of the International Committee of the Red Cross (ICRC), in his report on his visit to the camp on 17 November 1941, gives further detail: 'Planes dropped 176 incendiary bombs on the camp, which was almost completely burnt down.'

14 Officers, by provision of the Geneva Convention, were not allowed to work. A limited number of non-commissioned soldiers were allowed in Oflags to work as orderlies and perform services for the officers.

15 In his articles for *North American Newspaper Alliance*, 1945, Bader writes that Colonel George Young was '...an extremely good sapper...He had formed his own commando unit in the Middle East, which he led through the Abyssinian campaign and later landed on Crete in the final stages of that debâcle, as a result of which he became a prisoner of war. George Young fought the Germans at Lübeck - as far as it is possible for any senior British officer who is in prison behind barbed wire and has no arms nor, in the Germans eyes, right to fight.'

16 Bader states in *North American Newspaper Alliance*, 1945: 'The German ration actually was stolen by the Germans before it came to be issued to us.'

17 As Slavs, Russians were considered *'utermenschen'*, or 'subhuman' by the Germans. In the summer of 1941, thousands of Russian (Soviet) POWs were sent to camps specifically for them. Many of these POWs were civilians who had never seen military service, but Nazi policy in occupied territory was to treat all men between the ages of 15 and 65 as POWs. Thousands were dead on arrival at these camps. The rest were packed into the camps and left under an open sky without shelter. There, thousands more died of disease. Those who survived were beaten, abused and starved. Nearly two million Russians died in these camps. According to Joseph Goebbels, the German Minister for Propaganda and Public Information, as 'the Soviet Union had not signed the (Geneva) Convention and did not follow its provisions at all,' the law of war did not apply to them.

18 Menda, Casdagli's only sister, had married Anthony Lykiard and moved to Athens. In 1940, she had a son, also called Alexis. They were trapped by the Occupation, in the city. There was a famine in Greece; Athens was particularly badly affected. People were dying of hunger openly in the streets of the city. During this period of mass starvation, known as ο Μεγάλος Λιμός (the Great Famine), which lasted until 1944, an estimated 300,000 people died, but mortality rates peaked during the very bitter winter of 1941-2.

19 To lodge soldiers in a particular place, especially a civilian's house requisitioned for that purpose.

20 In his report on his visit to the camp, dated 17 November 1941, Dr Rubli

of the ICRC, writes, 'It seems that following this event (of the fire caused by bombing), the Protecting Power demanded that the British prisoners be transferred to another camp. They all have been moved to Oflag VI-B.'

Oflag VI-B, Dössel-Warburg
6. Fuck Hitler!

1 Adolf Hitler was the Leader of the National Socialist Germany Workers' Party (Nazi Party) from 1921 to 1945; the Chancellor of Germany from 1933 to 1945; and consolidated his power in 1934 to become the Führer of Germany until 1945. His rise to power directly precipitated the Second World War, the estimated death toll of which ranges from 60 to 85 million people, if the deaths from war-related disease and famine are included and those of at least 5 million prisoners of war (POWs). Hitler ordered the Holocaust in which 11-14 million people were killed, 6 million of whom were Jewish. On 30 April 1945, in Berlin, he committed suicide in an underground shelter or bunker by swallowing cyanide and then firing a bullet into his head. A week later, Germany signed an unconditional surrender bring the Second World War in Europe to an end.

2 The direct distance between Lübeck and Dössel is 250 miles. This journey was almost 640 miles long as having gone south to Buchen from Buchen they went north to Altenbeken and then back south to Warburg and so on to Dössel.

3 Dr Exchaquet, in his 15 October 1941 report on Oflag VI-B, for the International Committee of the Red Cross (ICRC), describes the room as follows: 'One room, occupied by 16 majors, has 8 doubled up bunks beds, 16 stools, a table where 12 people at most can sit, two double wardrobes, which means one half of a wardrobe per 4 officers.'

4 In fact, the officers crawled through a ventilator and dropped to the ground while the train was moving. One officer fell under the train's wheels to his death. When the train stopped, shots were fired and another officer was immediately recaptured. Among the four who escaped was the extraordinary Flt Lt Peter Stevens, who was born Georg Franz Hein in Hanover and became the only known German Jewish bomber pilot to bomb his own country. Stevens was later caught and sent to Oflag VI-B, his original destination. In 1945, he was awarded Britain's Military Cross for his numerous escape activities, of which this was the first. Also aboard the train that night was Sqn Ldr Roger Joyce Bushell, RAF. Later that night, when the train stopped briefly in Hanover, Bushell and another officer jumped from the train and

escaped, unnoticed by the German guards. They made their way to Prague but, in May 1942, were arrested and sent back to Germany. Bushell was to go on to mastermind the famous escape from Stalag Luft III, which inspired the film *The Great Escape* (1963). He was killed for his part in the operation by the Gestapo on 29 March 1944, aged 33. After the war, his killers were tried and executed by the Allies for this war crime.

5   Dr Exchaquet's report for the ICRC of 15 October 1941 states that there were 2,418 British officers in the camp and 446 orderlies.

6   General Victor Fortune – a splendid example of nominative determinism – was the Senior British Officer of all British prisoners in Europe, constituting some 200,000 officers and men. He had served with great distinction when commanding the 51st Highland Division, fighting a valiant rear-guard action at St Valery in 1940. Although the Highlanders were willing to fight to victory or death, General Fortune understood that, with the French Army collapsing around them, such sacrifice would be pointless. On 12 June 1940, in an act of great personal courage, he sought and obtained the approval of London to order his men to surrender. He was taken into captivity with his troops and worked tirelessly to improve their conditions with unfaltering continued resistance to the Germans.

7   Dr Exchaquet's report for the ICRC of his visit to Oflag VI-B on 15 October 1941 states: 'This camp is by far the worst we have seen in Germany. It is insufficient in every regard, and it seems impossible to us that even with months of methodical work, it could ever be brought into a state of providing its current contingent of prisoners with the most basic of living conditions. Winter is coming, and if the British prisoners remain in the camp, they will suffer badly in these conditions. Their soldiers' dignity has already suffered cruelly from the humiliating treatment imposed on them.'

8   The solitary confinement cells of a camp.

9   Carl worked at Emmanuel Casdagli & Sons for almost 50 years, keeping the books and records. He was also involved in the daily trading of cotton, wool and other commodities at Royal Exchange in Manchester.

10 On 4 September 1939, the RAF carried out the first raid of the Second World War by bombing warships in the Kiel Canal. The canal opened into the Baltic Sea and was one of the most strongly fortified positions in German territory. The raid, which was conducted in daylight, was not successful; the bombs were dropped from too low an altitude for their delayed-action fuses to detonate. Two aircraft were lost, with the resulting deaths of all

five members of their crews. Three other participants in the raid were taken prisoner, including Sgt L. J. Slattery, who suffered a dislocated jaw when the plane he was in crashed.

11 A Protecting Power is a state which protects another state and/or represents the interests of the protected state's citizens in a third state. At this time, the protecting powers included Switzerland, the United States of America and Portugal.

12 On 9 December 1941, the camp was again visited by the ICRC, this time by Dr Junod who reports: 'Before arriving at the British camp, we passed, on our right, some huts where approximately 300 Russian prisoners of war are interned. They are dressed in French uniforms, Serbian, Belgian; all quite disparate.'

13 Degrees of frost Fahrenheit (°F) are used to express cold, specifically how many degrees the air is below the freezing point of water. 19½ °F is equivalent to -12°C.

14 An ironic French expression meaning 'we shall see'.

15 On the morning of 7 December 1941, the Imperial Japanese Navy launched a surprise attack on the American naval base at Pearl Harbour in Hawaii, sinking five battleships, damaging 16 more and destroying almost 200 aircraft. More than 2,400 Americans were killed and over 1,000 injured in exchange for very light Japanese casualties. The next day, the United States declared war on Japan and entered the Second World War.

16 Sqn Ldr A. D. Murray, DFC of 73 Squadron Royal Air Force Akrotiri.

17 Here, for the first time, are the slanting lantern-like shapes that reoccur time and again in the embroideries. They are distaffs – spindles on which to wind flax or wool – and represent symbolically not only the materials used in the embroidery but also the family business of growing and trading in cotton and wool. The emblems of the four warring nations at the time, the British lion, the Russian hammer and sickle, the German swastika and the Italian eagle, are also shown. Surrounding them, in the narrow outer are the letters 'FUCKHITLER' in Morse code four and a half times; and in the inner border, 'GODSAVETHEKING' three times. Although the embroidery was pinned up in various prison rooms, the Germans never noticed the hidden messages it contained. The embroidery was exhibited in The Power of Making exhibition (Exhibit 91) at the Victoria & Albert Museum in London between September 2011 and January 2012.

7. Christmas 1941

1   The alcohol was usually a kind of 'moonshine' or *potcheen*, made by boiling up potatoes, adding sugar and then fermenting it. It was so potent it could take the enamel off the inside of a bucket.

2   In the bitterly cold winter of 1941-42, mortality rates among Russian POWs (whose numbers were already reduced by starvation and disease) sometimes went as high as 95 per cent. They were buried in mass graves.

3   The truss cost £3 in 1941, (equivalent to £128.25 in 2012 value).

4   A cutting from an unknown British newspaper, early January 1942, reads: 'OFLAG VI-B IMPROVEMENTS The War Office states that Oflag VI-B, which contains about 2,500 British officers and 470 orderlies, was visited on December 9 by a delegate of the International Red Cross Committee. Strong representations on the unsatisfactory features discovered were made immediately by the IRCC from Geneva and on the spot to the German authorities, who gave assurances that improvements would be made at once. These improvements, it is stated, have already started; 200 senior officers are now being transferred to a new camp and 400 airmen are to be transferred in the middle of January. Ten new brick barracks are being built. Food parcels are abundant and there is a very large stock in reserve. The prisoners were stated to be looking very fit and those from Greece and Crete to be very much improved in health.'

5   General Fortune was the SBO of the Upper Camp, Brigadier Somerset the SBO of the Lower Camp and Brigadier Nicholson the SBO of Oflag IX-A/Z, Rotenburg, 12½ miles away.

6   Casdagli and his sister, Menda, were keen skaters. As children, they skated as often as three times a week at the Manchester Ice Palace, which opened in 1910 and was for several years the only ice rink in England. Its magnificent facade was covered in marble; inside, the building had a vast hall for the ice rink, overlooked by a spacious balcony.

7   The sound of a drum or bugle, usually at daybreak, to wake soldiers up.

Oflag IX-A/H, Spangenberg
8. This Year, Next Year, Sometime...

1   Again the route was circuitous. The direct distance between Dössel and Elbersdorf is 55 miles. This route went west to Hofgeismar, then south to Malsfeld then due north again to Kassel and so on to Elbersdorf, a journey of 100 miles.

2   By Hugh Walpole. Published in 1930, *Herries Chronicle* tells the turbulent story of Francis Herries, his wife and family, the mistress he sells at a fair and of his great love for a teenage gypsy girl.

3   Casdagli was also working hard at something else. In early 1942, Lt Col. Swinburne, the security officer for Oflag IX-A/H, asked Casdagli if he would be prepared to be enrolled in the War Office code. This was for the British Directorate of Military Intelligence in the War Office, Section 9 (MI9), founded in December 1941 by Maj. Norman Crockatt. This small, dedicated, endlessly inventive team were responsible for escape and evasion. They aided resistance fighters; brought home Allied forces stranded or shot down behind enemy lines; and provided information and devices to POWs to help them escape, such as compasses hidden in tunic buttons and maps, printed on silk, disguised as handkerchiefs. Casdagli agreed. A few weeks later, Swinburne sent for him again and told him that, from then on, he would give him messages, from time to time, to encode in his letters home and instructed him in the working of the code. Casdagli continued working for MI9 until the end of the war.

4   Homer's epic poem *The Iliad* is one of the oldest extant works of Western literature. Set in the Trojan War, it tells the story of the battles and events between King Agamemnon and the warrior Achilles.

5   Casdagli spoke no German. This is his plural of *Frau*, German for 'woman'.

6   The Swiss Commission was a delegation of Swiss diplomatic officials, who, among other tasks, as representatives of the Swiss Government, inspected prisoners of war (POW) camps in various belligerent countries between 1939 and 1945.

7   Founded in London in 1844, the Young Men's Christian Association (YMCA) operates in 119 countries and reaches 58 million people. It works to bring social justice and peace to young people and their communities, regardless of religion, race, gender or culture. During the Second World War, the YMCA supported thousands of POWs in many different countries and Japanese-Americans in internment camps by sending sports equipment, clothing and educational materials to prisoners and arranging for sports to be played in the camps.

8   Theo was Casdagli's youngest brother; £1,500 was equivalent to £280,000 in 2012 value.

9   Petit point is also known as tent stitch, needlepoint and half-cross stitch. It is

much finer than cross stitch as only one thread of the canvas is embroidered with one slanting stitch whereas in cross-stitch two threads are embroidered with two slanting stitches.

10 The Latin quote on the bookmark Casdagli embroidered for his birthday is from Virgil and translates: 'O that Jupiter would give me back the years that are gone!'

11 The Swiss Legation is another name for the Swiss Commission. (See endnote 6 of this chapter).

12 An extract from a letter to General Kaffatos from the POW Dept. of Greek Red Cross, Athens, dated 19 March 1942 and received at Oflag IX-A/H on 5 April 1942, states 'Our office has been investigating your case since July 1941. According to a declaration from the German Red Cross, you are the only Greek Prisoner of War in Germany today. We naturally tried to find out why you were being so treated, since the Leader of the German People has said that no Greeks would be kept prisoner. Your captivity is the result, neither of a mistake nor due to carelessness. As the German Red Cross told us: "General Kaffatos is being held, not as a Greek prisoner, but a British one."' The letter is signed by A. Thiakakis and S. Mavrocordato and was translated by Casdagli.

13 Stump or prison cricket, played with ball, wicket and stumps improvised from oddments by the prisoners with 'captive' inventiveness and involving elaborate systems of boundaries.

14 Aidan Crawley was at Harrow with Casdagli. They shared the same birthday and he, like Casdagli, was a great cricketer. He was shot down over Italy in 1941. After the war, he wrote '*Escape from Germany*' (London, HMSO, 1985), was an MP for both Labour and Conservatives, Editor-In-Chief of *Independent Television News*, Chairman of London Weekend Television and was made an Officer of the Order of the British Empire (OBE). In 1985, he remembered Casdagli at Spangenberg 'as always smiling and glad to be alive'.

15 A national day of remembrance in Australia and New Zealand commemorating all Australians and New Zealanders who have served and died in wars, conflicts, and peacekeeping operations.

16 Parole agreements are promises a person gives their captor to fulfil stated conditions, such as not to bear arms or not to escape, in consideration of special privileges, such as release from captivity or temporary or lessened restraint.

17 The moat was filled with boulders, rubbish and fetid debris of all kinds, and it stank. It was said to be inhabited by three wild bears, nicknamed 'Gustave and his two wives'.

18 Mrs Hamson, née Thérèse Gabrielle Boudon, was a spirited, charming French woman and devoted wife and mother. Jack and Casdagli had persuaded their mothers (Jack's in Turkey and Casdagli's in Cairo) to send them both parcels.

19 Roger Elletson had been with Casdagli in Crete and was captured there. He was one of the officers taken ill on the cattle truck journey from the Aegean to the Baltic and was now in Elbersdorf, the lower camp of Oflag IX-A/H.

20 Gambling was a common pastime in every camp. While it was a great way of relieving the boredom of prison, in some camps it got out of hand, with officers finding themselves in serious debt and attempts, not always successful, were made by Senior British Officers (SBOs) to regulate it.

21 About four pounds and twelve shillings or £4.60 (the equivalent to £185.60 in 2012 value).

22 Theodosiades was a Commander with 335th Hellenic Squadron which was part of RAF Fighter Command. Formed in late 1941, the Squadron, whose call sign was 'Tigers', were based in El Daba, Egypt. From there, they flew fighter patrols over the Western (Libyan) Desert. Theodosiades was shot down during one such operation in early 1942 and taken prisoner. As soon as he was repatriated to Athens, Theodosiades re-joined his Squadron and later that year took part in the Squadron's most audacious raid. On 28 October 1942, 'Oxi' (Οχι) Day, the second anniversary of Greece's entry into war and of the Italian invasion of Greece, they flew behind enemy lines and successfully bombed the Italian Headquarters.

23 Military slang for being in prison, from 'to bag' or 'secure'.

24 This writing becomes the first two chapters of this diary.

25 The Geneva Convention provided that badly injured or severely ill POWs and those showing signs of mental illness should be sent back to their own country. The Repatriation Board, also called the Repatriation Commission or Committee, considered each case of a POW seeking repatriation on medical grounds. It was made up of three doctors: two from a neutral country, usually Switzerland, and one from the imprisoning country. Their decisions were made by majority.

26   The Libyan port of Tobruk, near the Egyptian border, was the best natural harbour in North Africa and of great strategic importance. On 21 June 1942, it fell to the Axis forces in a surprise attack led by Field Marshal Rommel, known as the Desert Fox for his skill in desert warfare. Over 30,000 Allied troops were taken prisoner.

27   These officers were British Commandos. The Commandos were a revolutionary new concept in soldiering. All were volunteers for special service. They had to be highly intelligent, fit, independently-minded, and above all, supremely tough. They were then trained in 'the butcher and bolt' approach to operations and in 'thinking outside the box'. On 27 March 1942, when the fortunes of the Allied forces were at an all-time low, they carried out the daring, brilliant and supposedly impossible St Nazaire Raid or, as it became known, the Greatest Raid of All. That night, they sailed the HMS *Campbeltown*, an obsolete destroyer hastily disguised as a German warship and packed with explosives, from Falmouth to the largest dry dock in the world at St Nazaire in occupied France. St Nazaire was targeted because the loss of its dry dock would force any large German warship, such as the battleship *Tirpitz*, if it were in need of repairs, to return to home waters rather than having the safe haven of St Nazaire available to it on the Atlantic coast. With immense courage and under the eyes and fire of the Germans, the Commandos succeeded in ramming *Campbeltown* into the massive metal dock gates. At noon the next day, it exploded, destroying the dry dock and surrounding U-boat installations. Only 228 of the force of 622 returned to Britain; 169 were killed and 215 became prisoners of war. Five Victoria Crosses were won on the raid, the largest number ever awarded for a single action.

28   Anthony Lykiard, Menda's husband.

29   Two large camps were located at Biberach in south Germany: Oflag V-B and Ilag V-B, an internment camp for Allied civilians, mainly from the Channel Islands.

30   The President of the Mess Committee (PMC) is the senior officer elected by the mess membership to run the Mess' affairs.

31   'This year, next year, sometime, never' is a traditional English counting game played with objects such as prune stones or daisy petals to divine the future.

9. The Strange Freedom of Clouds

1   A person with the duty of collecting excise, as in Customs and Excise.

2   Rodney Gee was a veteran of both World Wars and captured in both. Before the war, he was the housemaster of Dakyns' at Clifton and after liberation in 1945, returned to Clifton to become housemaster of Watson's. During his time as a POW, he produced and directed plays by Shakespeare.

3   Majors W. E. Pearson (Bill) and C. E. Hamilton-Stewart (Hamill) and Lt E. A. Rée were also in Room 13.

4   The German authorities withheld all mail, outgoing and incoming, to Oflag IX-A/H from August to October 1942 (inclusive) in reprisal for mail to German POWs in the Far East allegedly not being properly organised.

5   At Harrow School, Casdagli participated in House Singing (1923-4); House Madrigals, the School Choir and School Singing XII (1924); and the School Musical Society (1925).

6   Lt John Bourlon de Pree of 2nd Battalion, Seaforth Highlanders, died on 30 August 1942, aged 24 and is buried in the Hanover War Cemetery, Germany.

7   *Grand Blessés* were severely injured POWs; *Lessés Légers* were those with minor injuries.

8   Oflag IX-A/Z, formerly Oflag IX-C, was in the small town of Rotenburg an de Fulda, 13 miles south of Oflag IX-A/H.

9   H(is) M(ajesty's) T(roopship) *Pasteur*, built by the French and named after their famous scientist Louis Pasteur, was originally designed as a luxury liner for 751 passengers. In 1942, the *Pasteur* was converted into a troopship. As she was the third-fastest ship of her time, she normally made her crossings alone, without a warship escort.

10   Oflag IX-A/H may have been singled out for reprisals because of the presence of General Fortune, the SBO in Germany.

11   After his failed escape from the Lower Camp on 24 May 1942, Peter Dollar was moved to the more secure Upper Camp. '*Terror Angriffe*' is German for 'Terror Attacks'.

12   Casdagli's Rolex was an Oyster Imperial Chronometre, Watch No: 127573 and it came with a letter from Hans Wilsdorf, the founder of Rolex Watches, to say payment was not due until after the war. Casdagli was one of at least 3,000 recipients of such wartime Rolexes. Hans Wilsdorf was born in Bavaria, Germany but in 1905, aged 24, he went to London and set up his own watch-making business and created Rolex as a brand for selling his

watches. During the First World War, he moved to Switzerland where, in 1920, he established Montres Rolex. By the start of the Second World War, Rolex watches had acquired a fine reputation for their precision and as luxury time-pieces. When Wilsdorf learnt that captured Allied forces were having their Rolex watches confiscated or stolen from them by the Germans, he made the British POWs among them an offer: if they wrote and told him of the circumstances of their loss, he would replace their lost Rolex with a new one, with payment not due until after the war.

13 On 19 August 1942, over 2,000 Allied troops, mainly Canadian, were taken prisoner during Operation Jubilee in a disastrous seaborne raid on the German-occupied French port of Dieppe. The Germans alleged that during this action, a number of their troops taken prisoner by the Allied forces had been tied up and that unless an apology was forthcoming, all the Canadian and British prisoners taken at Dieppe would be tied up in reprisal. The British government did not apologise and warned that, if their POWs were bound, an equal number of German POWs would be too. By noon on 8 October, over 1,300 Canadian and British POWs were shackled and paraded in their camps.

14 On 10 October 1942, the War Office had made the following announcement: 'The German Government having put into operation the illegal action threatened in their communiqué, the War Office announces that unless the German Government releases prisoners captured at Dieppe from their chains, an equal number of German prisoners will be manacled and chained at noon on October 10th.' The Germans did not comply but instead retaliated by chaining at least twice as many Canadian and British POWs. Mediation by the International Committee of the Red Cross (ICRC) ameliorated the situation several weeks later, but it took over a year before the reprisals on both sides ended completely.

15 The Repatriation Commission, also called the Repatriation Board or Committee, considered each case of a POW seeking repatriation on medical grounds. It was made up of three doctors: two from a neutral country, usually Switzerland, and one from the imprisoning country. Their decisions were made by majority.

16 The Hamson family, who were jewel merchants and had been for generations, lived in Istanbul but were not Turkish.

17 The phosphorescent light was probably given off by bioluminescent fungi on decaying wood, such as *armillaria melleam* which emits a bluish-green

luminosity. The fungus is a pathogen which can decimate whole forests leaving behind it 'ghost trees'.

18 Now known as Remembrance or Poppy Day, Armistice Day was first commemorated at the end of the First World War in 1919, as a memorial day for the Armed forces who died in the line of duty. Every year, at the eleventh hour of the eleventh day of the eleventh month, two minutes of silence are observed and wreaths are laid at war monuments.

19 The Repatriation Committee, see endnote 15 of this chapter.

20 The Swiss Legation's report of 26 November 1942 stated: 'The spirit is splendid. The sight of nearly four hundred bearded officers in plain uniform is of course shocking, but the air of manliness and dignity with which they bear themselves makes a great impression on everybody.'

10. Charming People

1 The Channel Islands were invaded by Germany on 30 June 1940 and were the only part of the UK occupied by Nazi forces. In 1942, the German authorities announced that all British subjects on the Channel Islands without permanent residence papers would be deported; in September, 2,200 islanders were taken to Germany and interned for the duration of the war. They were mainly held at Ilag V-B in Biberach, an internment camp for Allied civilians.

2 Hooch or hootch is illicit, inferior or home-brewed alcoholic liquor. It gets its name from the Alaskan liquor-making tribe, the Hoochinoo.

3 On Christmas Eve 1942, Operation Winter Storm, a German offensive to break the Soviet encirclement of the bulk of the German 6th Army (over 250,000 men), which was trapped inside Stalingrad failed; by Christmas Day, the 4th Panzer Army was in full retreat. Hitler is said to have hated Stalingrad because it was named after the Russian leader, Joseph Stalin. On 17 July 1942, the Nazis bombed it, precipitating the Battle of Stalingrad, one of the bloodiest and most brutal battles in the Second World War.

4 Although he didn't talk much, Casdagli had a beautiful speaking voice. But that is not why he would have made an appropriate radio announcer. Most camps had at least one clandestine wireless radio set. At Oflag IX-A/H, the wireless was in Casdagli's room, Room 13, hidden under the floorboards under the window, according to his embroidery, *Room 13*. Wirelesses and wireless parts were smuggled into camp by MI9 or MIS-X,

America's counterpart secret agency. Whether 'home-made' or smuggled in, wirelesses in prisons were almost invariably receivers, not transmitters, used by prisoners to follow the events of the war and also as a means to receive coded messages. Every Wednesday the BBC broadcast *Good Evening Forces* in which the Rev. Selby-Wright, known as 'the Radio Padre', gave a short moralistic talk; the programme had approximately seven million listeners worldwide. Encoded in the talks were messages from the War Office. 'When I began a talk with "Good Evening Forces"', Selby-Wright later explained, 'it meant I was going to code my talk for a bit and when I came to the word "but" it meant it was finished.' As Casdagli was in MI9 and enrolled in the War Office code, he was almost certainly involved in writing down the coded messages, deciphering them and then 'announcing' their contents.

5 A sport similar to bowls or *boule* in which players slide stones across ice towards a target area. In 1942, the Royal Caledonian Curling Club received a request from General Fortune for curling stones to be sent to the Upper Camp of Oflag IX-A/H. Sixteen stones were duly despatched and sent to the camp via the International Red Cross Committee and the British Consul in Geneva. In a letter dated 2 July 1945, General Fortune recalled, 'During the winter of 1943-44, we had about 26 days' curling; during the winter of 1944-45 we had about 30 days' curling.'

6 The prisoners must have been listening to their wireless radios. That day, against Hitler's orders, Field Marshall Paulus surrendered to the Russians and the 91,000 German troops trapped in the city were taken prisoner. Within a matter of weeks, over a quarter of them were dead; less than 6,000 survived the Soviet labour camps and returned to Germany after the war. The Battle of Stalingrad is considered by many to have been the turning point of the Second World War in Europe as, having sustained such a massive loss, the Germans could not stop the Russian advance to Germany.

7 Matches were sometimes worth more in the camp markets than cigarettes. They were valued not just because they were sometimes scarce but because they could be sharpened and used for cleaning teeth.

8 The *Völkischer Beobachter* was the daily newspaper of the Nationalist Socialist German Workers' Party (*Nationalsozialistische Deutsche Arbeiterpartei*), the political party founded in Germany in 1919 and brought to power by Hitler in 1933. The *Frankfurter Zeitung* was considered to be the only newspaper not completely controlled by Joseph Goebbels and his Ministry of Propaganda. It ceased publishing in 1943.

9 Newspaper was used for toilet paper.

10 Vasilli Naxakis and his wife, Crystalli, lived in Crete.

11 The world's first Rotary Club was founded in Chicago in 1905 by Paul P.H. Harris.

12 Judy was Joyce's sister.

13 John Sanderson Poole, known as Jack, was a veteran of the First World War in which he was captured three times. In the Second World War, he served with The King's Royal Rifle Corps and was taken prisoner at Calais in 1940. He told his colourful life story in his autobiography *Undiscovered Ends* (London, Cassell & Company Ltd, 1957).

14 Colditz Castle, situated on a rocky outcrop above the River Mulde, was thought to be escape-proof. In 1933, it was made into a prison camp for 'undesirables' such as communists, homosexuals and Jews. In 1939, it became Oflag IV-C, a *straffe-lager* or high security punishment camp for Allied POWs who were incorrigible escapers or regarded as particularly dangerous.

15 Oflag VII-C was in a square 15th century castle in Laufen on the Bavarian and Austrian border. In May 1942, it became Ilag VII, an internment camp for Channel Islands deportees. It also housed American civilians captured in Europe in December 1941 when Germany declared war on America.

16 Stalag VIII-B, Lamsdorf was one of the best equipped hospitals of all Stalags. It had X-ray facilities, operating theatres and laboratories, and was entirely staffed by prisoners working under a German Colonel doctor. It later became Stalag 344.

17 Cannibalism amongst desperate Russian POWs was deliberately encouraged by the Nazis, who held it up to their own people as an example of the behaviour of sub-humans who could never be like civilised human beings.

18 Ten days earlier, on 6 March 1943, in an offensive called Operation Capri, Axis forces had attacked the northernmost British strongpoint, territory towards the Tunisian city of Medenine. The British forced them to retreat destroying 55 of their tanks in the process. Three days later, Rommel, the commander of Army Group Africa, left Tunisia for Germany to try to personally persuade Hitler to withdraw from Tunisia and deploy those troops in Europe. Hitler not only refused but replaced Rommel who was never to return to Africa again.

19 Casdagli's mother was still living in Cairo although, after her husband's

death in 1942, the Villa Casdagli had been sold. In 1943, the Villa Casdagli became the American Embassy for the duration of the Second World War. In 1952, it was turned into a girls' school and fell into some neglect. In 2006, the Supreme Council of Antiquities listed the Villa Casdagli as a heritage site and an Islamic monument. In 2008, in collaboration with the United States Agency for International Development and the American Research Centre in Cairo, its restoration was planned, to be funded by the US Department of State's Ambassadors Fund for Cultural Preservation. The Villa Casdagli was to become a museology institute with a public library. In 2010, the girls' school was duly relocated so that preparations could begin to restore the Villa's unique architectural features. On 1 February 2013, during a period of political turmoil in the city, the Villa Casdagli was looted, torched by rioters and left in ruins.

20 Despite the difference in age, Catherine Casdagli and Michael Parish became great friends and stayed in touch until her death.

21 Horlicks tablets were made from malted milk and fortified with vitamins and minerals. On the tin, it said: 'As used by Explorers and Long Distance Flyers. As supplied to the Air Ministry'.

22 Alan 'Black' Campbell and Jimmy Yule were in rooms next to each other and were great friends. They took a door off its hinges so that their neighbours could come in and play cards with them. Their attempted escape failed when they were captured crossing the castle moat.

23 Chaplain Steven Kane, a Roman Catholic priest who held Catholic and Protestant services, was considered hardworking, inspirational and a pillar of morale.

11. Rest in Peace

1 A nark was a spy or 'stool pigeon' who tried to trick information out of prisoners. The Military Intelligence Service's *Intelligence Bulletin* for December 1942 states: 'A soldier is still a soldier for his country after capture. Except to give his name, rank, and serial number, absolutely no other questions should be answered. According to the instructions given by both the Axis and United Nations under international law, no other information is required.'

2 'Herr' Detmering was Commander Rolf Detmering. According to *The Records of The United States Nuremberg War Crimes Trials Interrogations*, Commander Rolf Detmering was interrogated by the Office of the Chief Counsel for War Crimes (OCCWC) on 14, 16 and 17 July 1947.

3   In April 1943, the bodies of almost 4,500 Polish officers and nationals were discovered by the Nazis in mass graves in the forest of Katyn near Smolensk, an area formerly in Russia but now in German hands. Virtually without exception, execution had been by a single bullet to the back of the head and many of the dead had their hands tied behind their backs. The corpses were piled face down on top of each other, six or seven layers deep. The compacted clay soil had kept the bodies and clothing almost whole. Lt Col. Van Vliet, who was forced to go Katyn by the Germans, wrote in his witness testimony of 4 February 1952 to the Select Committee on the Katyn Forest Massacre (Washington): 'A sickly-sweet odour of decaying bodies was everywhere. At the graves it was nearly overpowering.' The massacre had taken place April 1940 at a time when the Germans and Russians were allies. By April 1943, the Russians were fighting on the side of the Allied forces; the Germans wanted to blame the Allies for the massacre and, through this powerful propaganda victory, set the Allies against each other. Russia was equally determined to blame the Nazis for the atrocity. As well as at Katyn, executions took place simultaneously at the nearby Kozelsk prisoner of war camp, in the camps of Starobelsk and Ostashkov, in Smolensk itself, at prisons in Kalinin, Kharkiv, Moscow and other Soviet cities and at various locations in Belarus. The final death toll of Polish officers and nationals massacred at Katyn and other similar sites between April and May 1940 was in excess of 21,000.

4   In late March 1943, the Allied 8th Army attacked the Axis forces on the Mareth line in Tunisia, North Africa, and drove them north. They also attacked from the west pushing the enemy up into Tunis and the coastal town of Bizerte. In the final assault on 7–9 May, the Allies entered Tunis and Bizerte respectively, declaring victory on 13 May and taking 275,000 prisoners.

5   At full moon on 16 to 17 May 1943, Operation Chastise, an attack on the dams of the Ruhr Valley, was successfully carried out by 617 Squadron, RAF Bomber Command, using the 'bouncing bomb', which was specially invented and developed by Barnes Wallis. Although the Sorpe dam was almost unscathed, the Möhne and Edersee dams were devastated, causing the catastrophic flooding of the Ruhr valley and villages in the Eder valley. Crucial factories and power plants were destroyed and an estimated 1,600 people were drowned, including about 700 forced labourers from occupied countries and Soviet prisoners of war (POWs). Of the 19 Lancaster bombers involved in the raid, only 11 returned home; 53 aircrew out of 133 died and three were taken prisoner. *The Dam Busters*, a film based on these events, was made in 1955 and was the most popular film of that year.

6   Lt Col. Guy Johnson German of the Royal Leicestershire Regiment was captured in Norway on 23 April 1940. He was the first Senior British Officer at Colditz, from 1941 to 1942, and an inveterate escaper and defiant prisoner.

7   'Oh shit!'

8   All three officers sent to Katyn were from Oflag IX-A/Z Rotenburg. Lt Col. Stevenson RAMC, a British Officer from South Africa, was the senior of the three. The other two were Americans, Capt. Donald Stewart and Lt Col. Van Vliet, who was the Senior Allied Officer (SAO) for the 125 American prisoners in Oflag IX-A/Z, a predominantly British camp. They viewed the masses graves and the exhumations of the bodies on 13 May 1943 and were each given by the Germans a set of photographs documenting the visit.

9   The Russians, under the dictatorship of Joseph Stalin, were guilty of the Katyn massacres. The Soviet Union continued to deny this until 1990, when it officially acknowledged that the massacre had been carried out by the Soviet secret police, the People's Commissariat for Internal Affairs (NKVD). By the time Stalin died in 1953, he had been responsible for the deaths of over 20 million people.

10 An extract from the *Public Record Office WO 373/100*, London states: 'Major CASDAGLI was captured at Sphakia, CRETE on 1 June 41. Two months later he was transferred to Germany. Although he was not sufficiently fit to try to escape he helped to dig a tunnel in August [sic] 43 at SPANGENBERG (OFLAG IX A/H).' Escape from the impregnable fortress of Spangenberg was almost impossible, yet the team of tunnelers planned an escape by digging a tunnel under the moat of the castle. The first task was to sink a shaft below the level of the deep moat but during this work, their tunnel was discovered.

11 Guy German was sent back to Colditz again. On his release in April 1945 he was awarded the DSO.

12 Casdagli's younger brother.

13 Brigadier Claude Nicholson CB, known as the Defender of Calais, was the SBO of Oflag IX-A/Z, Rotenburg, and had previously been the SBO of Oflag VII-C, Lufen. He was the second most senior officer of all British POWs in Germany and one of the most talented and popular soldiers of his generation. Nicholson was in command at the Siege of Calais on 22 to 26 May 1940 and, against overwhelming odds, bravely and tenaciously, defended the port for the three days of desperate fighting. This allowed the Allies to consolidate their hold on Dunkirk 27 miles away and carry out

its evacuation. When Calais fell on 26 May, Nicholson, along with 3,500 British soldiers and many thousands of other Allied forces, was taken prisoner. In captivity, he suffered from ill health. Shortly before his death, he and Lt Col. Van Vliet, the SAO at Rotenburg, had protested to the Swiss Protecting Power that officers from the camp should not to be forced to view the exhumations of the mass graves of murdered Polish officers at Katyn but they were not successful. Nicholson's is the only soldier's grave in the Rotenburg Civil Cemetery. At home, he was an accomplished horseman and stood to inherit Maperton House in Somerset from his aunt, where he had spent many happy times and was well liked and respected locally. He was husband to Hon. Ursula Katharine Hanbury-Tracy, and had two children, Richard Hugh and Sylvia Mary Victoria. Nicholson, who died aged 45, probably as the result of suicide, was posthumously made a Companion of the Order of the Bath.

12. Four Years of War

1   The 'hole in the wall' was the cache for secret documents. In less than a month, the Germans had found the tunnel, the wireless and the hiding place for secret documents and other materials. Jack Poole, in *Undiscovered Ends* (London, Cassell & Company Ltd, 1957) said that this was no ordinary coincidence and he was certain the prisoners were being betrayed. A newly- arrived British NCO, who had posed as an officer at another camp, was suspected of being a Nazi 'stooge' or traitor. After the discoveries at Spangenberg, this man was transferred to Oflag IX-A/Z Rotenberg from which, a short while later, he was again summarily removed. After his departure, a search was made by the Germans who immediately found the camp's tunnel.

2   Founded in 1928, the Squash Rackets Association took over the administration of squash in Britain from the Tennis and Rackets Association. Casdagli was an early and lifelong member.

3   Flying Fortresses or Boeing B-17s were four-engined heavy bombers operated by the US Army Air Corps and used for precision daylight bombing. The US 8th Air Force flew these bombing raids over Germany from bases in Britain.

4   Benito Mussolini founded Fascism in Italy, an extreme authoritarian and nationalistic form of government, and was the country's dictator for over two decades. After the Allies landed on the Italian island of Sicily on 9 July 1943, the Fascist Party voted for Mussolini's retirement but Mussolini refused to go. On 25 July 1943, after another vote, King Victor Emmanuel III had

Mussolini arrested and imprisoned. The Germans helped him to escape and he went to northern Italy to try to regain power. On 28 April 1945, two days before Hitler's death, Mussolini was caught by communist partisans while attempting to flee to safety in Switzerland. He and 14 other members of his party, including his mistress, Clara Petacci, were executed by firing squad. The corpses were taken to Milan where seven of them, including those of Mussolini and Petacci, were hung by their feet from the girder of an Esso petrol station in the Piazzale Loreto and their bodies were mutilated by the angry crowd.

5   The Camp Commandant's Office.

6   A power of attorney is a legal document giving another person the authority to act on one's behalf in legal or financial matters. Hargrove, Casdagli's friend from Harrow School, was his solicitor and looking after his affairs while he was in prison, as Hargrove was a non-combatant. Hargrove's wife was killed in the London Blitz some time before Casdagli gave him this power of attorney.

7   On 3 September 1943, the Italian government and the Allies signed the Armistice of Cassibile in which Italy totally capitulated and left the Axis forces. The Armistice was publicly announced five days later.

8   These 'rest camps', better known as 'holiday camps', were purportedly camps for long-term prisoners to have a rest from barbed wire for one month and enjoy 'German kindness and goodwill'. In reality, they were indoctrination and propaganda camps created by the Waffen SS in 1943 to recruit British POWs into a unit called the British Free Corps (BFC) whose mission was to fight against the Allies, particularly the Soviets. There were two 'holiday camps' in the southern suburbs of Berlin, both sub-camps of Stalag III-D. One was Special Detachment 999 for officers; the second, only a short distance away, was Special Detachment 517, Genshagen, for other ranks, where the POWs were given free beer, entertainment, trips to Berlin on parole, black-market Red Cross goods and even had their own café. These efforts to recruit members of the Allied forces into the BFC were almost wholly unsuccessful. In total, during the whole period of their existence, the BFC numbered less than sixty men.

9   Maj. Robin Snook and Capt. Richard (Dick) Lorraine hatched an impossible plan for a daylight escape. They were assisted by Maj. Jack Poole and a team of twenty POWs. Poole describes the procedure in *Undiscovered Ends* (London, Cassell & Company Ltd, 1957), although he gets the date wrong.

Preparations included ropes and a rope ladder, a hook and pulley, German-speaking prisoners, shouts of 'yellow', a red book and green shirt, flute-playing and a cocoa tin suspended on black thread. On 3 October 1943, a rope with a hook was thrown 30 feet across the moat and the hook caught a railing; Snook and Lorraine slid down a rope from the castle, ran across the moat, pulled up the rope ladder, scrambled up the ladder and escaped as the rope and ladder were swiftly hidden. The escape took less than five minutes; some cunning deceptions by the other POWs successfully covered the escapees' absence, giving them a forty-eight hours' start.

10 Attacked repeatedly with bombs or machine-gun fire from low-flying aircraft.

11 Darmstadt is 125 miles south west of Spangenberg and about 150 miles from the French border.

12 Oflag VII.B Eichstätt was about 62 miles north of Munich in Bavaria.

13 This would seem unlucky as, a week before, on 13 October 1943, and a month after its surrender to the Allies, Italy switched sides and declared war on Nazi Germany, its former partner.

14 Lt Col. Willie Tod was the last SBO at Oflag IV-C, where he was again respected and admired for his courage and affability.

15 Casdagli spent virtually nothing on himself in captivity but saved everything for his wife and son. His 'pay' was 54 marks a month, equivalent to £3 and 10 shillings or £3.50. The sum he sent home from his prison 'pay' was equivalent to his 'pay' for 46 months, but, as he had only been in prison for 42 months, he must have also had savings, credit or money on him when captured, or he sold or traded some of his possessions or worked for others.

16 The Greek island of Cos, or Κως, was an Italian province. When Italy surrendered to the Allies, the British and Germans fought for control of the island. The Battle of Cos took place on 3 October 1943. The Germans won and occupied the island until 1945 when it became a protectorate of the UK, which gave Cos to Greece in 1947.

17 Brigadier Robert Tilney was appointed Commander of the British forces on the Greek island of Leros (Λέρος) in the Dodecanese group of islands a week before the Battle of Leros began on 12th November 1943. Four days later, Tilney surrendered in one of the last great defeats of the Second World War for the British Army. He spent the rest of the war in prison and was later

awarded the DSO and made a CBE. Alistair MacLean's novel *The Guns of Navarone* was based on this battle; a film of the same name, made in 1961, starred Gregory Peck, David Niven and Anthony Quinn.

18 Menda and her family, like thousands of others in Athens, were suffering. The Occupation was over three years old. Her son, Alexis, was almost five. Conditions were worsening and the airports of Athens, Kalamaki, Eleusis and Tatoi had been heavily bombed by the Allies on 6, 8, 14 December 1943.

19 On 21 June 1939, *The Glasgow Herald* reported Herr Walther Rienhardt, the German Consul-General in Liverpool, had received instructions to be recalled to Berlin by the Nazi authorities. His departure followed a request by the British government, which believed Rienhardt was a spy and was implicated in 'the recent Chorley Official Secrets case'.

20 A French expression meaning 'too bad! ' or 'never mind! '

21 Lt Col. Barclay, in a talk after the war, described curling at Oflag IX-A/H: 'Our curling,' he states, 'of course, was carried out in a very restricted area in the moat of this old castle in which we lived. You will wonder how we managed that. There was no water in the moat and we had to beat down the snow to make a surface and water it every day and every evening until finally we got a skin of ice on it, and that was where we curled. Unfortunately, one end of the rink was about 2 feet lower than the other end, so you had to keep your hand in when curling down the hill. However, that worked quite well and we had some very good sport indeed. We used to be curling from half-past eight in the morning – that was when we were allowed out of our rooms – and it just went on all day, with a few battles with the people who wanted to skate, until nightfall.'

22 Long flights were impossible without extra fuel stored in 'drop tanks', which were generally attached to the bomb shackle on the wing. The tanks were dropped when empty, thus lightening the plane and allowing for greater manoeuvrability.

13. Per Anum Ad Astra

1 Latin for 'through the anus to the stars'. This is Casdagli's reworking of the motto of the RAF and of other Commonwealth air forces: '*per ardua ad astra*', meaning 'through struggle to the stars'.

2 On 4 April 1945, a few days after the prisoners left Oflag IX-A/H, Spangenberg Castle, it was bombed by the United States Army Air Corps

(USAAF). It remained a burnt-out shell until the late 1950s when it was rebuilt as a hotel. Until about 2006, Hotel Schloss Spangenberg was a four star gourmet hotel with conference facilities but no longer operates as a hotel.

3   *The Waddingtons Story* by Victor Watson, (Jeremy Mills Publishers, 2008) describes some ingenious ways in which Waddingtons helped to get maps into POW camps. Waddingtons had perfected printing on silk. In 1939, at the request of MI9, it printed maps on silk and hid them in games, often embedding them in Monopoly boards or minutely folding them inside Monopoly playing pieces. Games and pastimes were allowed in care parcels. These 'doctored' games were always sent in parcels from fake charities, such as the Licensed Victuallers Prisoner Relief Fund, but never in Red Cross parcels. Any discovery of escaping aids in Red Cross parcels could jeopardise it continuing to provide essential aid. Until 2007, Waddingtons' wartime activities were top secret and classified information under the British Official Secrets Act.

4   Sqn Ldr Aidan Crawley recalled after the war: 'As for the anal passage, as well as documents, we also carried compasses in it.'

5   Piles or haemorrhoids are swellings in the lining of the anus and lower rectum, which can be painful, inflamed and itchy.

6   The Sherwells were a famous South African sporting family. G.R. Sherwell frequently played at Wimbledon. Amongst other titles, T. Y. Sherwell won the Rogers Cup Men Singles in 1908 and 1914. Their brother, P.W. Sherwell, was the South African Cricket Captain.

7   Casdagli's uncle, Xenophon Casdagli, known as Uncle X, had died the year before on 2 May 1943, aged 63. He was a first-class tennis player. Amongst other prestigious matches, in 1906, he won a silver and bronze medal at the Olympic Games in Athens and at the All England Mixed Doubles with Mrs Cooper Sterry, the Wimbledon Ladies' Singles champion.

8   Giessen, written Gießen in German, was of strategic importance as a railway hub and a garrison town for 2,000 German troops. It was also the location of one of the 174 sub-camps of Bunchenwald in the town Weimar, 137 miles away, one of the first and largest concentration camps. At the Giessen sub-camp, surgical and chemical experiments were performed on human beings, many of whom died. In late 1944, Allied bombing destroyed three quarters of the town, including historic buildings and the north wing of the station.

OFLAG XII-B, HADAMAR
14. A Phobia of Barbed Wire

1   The camp at Hadamar opened in 1939 for Polish officers, numbered Oflag XII-A. In 1942, renumbered Oflag XII-B, it took in British, French and other Allied officers. After Italy's capitulation in 1943, POWs were transferred from Italy to Oflag XII-B where they were joined by volunteers from other camps.

2   These officers were Majors J.H. Darlow, C.H. Deighton, S. Griffith, C.J. Johansen, G.S. Johnson, W. Mantell-Harding, D. Patterson, R.J. Wilby, H. S. Wilson and Lt F. Rennie.

3   The Geneva Convention required POWs who died in captivity to be honourably buried in marked graves.

4   A hernia can strangulate when too much intestine comes through the gap in the muscle wall and becomes squeezed, cutting off blood supply to the portion of intestine in the hernia and causing severe pain. If not operated on, can, in rare cases, lead to death.

5   A spa town 46 miles southwest of Hadamar known for its springs and their beneficial mineral properties.

6   The Gestapo were the secret police force of the Nazi Party. They were empowered to torture prisoners, send people to concentration camps and to carry out many other ruthless acts in the name of protecting the German state.

7   The holiday camp for officers had been moved from the suburbs of Berlin to Schloss Steinburg on the fringes of the Bavarian forests. In *Detour* (London, The Falcon Press, 1946), Lt Stewart Walker writes of being ordered to go there by the Germans from Oflag IX-A/H, Spangenberg at exactly this time, May 1944. It was, he reports, a comfortable white mansion in its own grounds for 50 officers guarded by four sentries. The camp was on parole all day but not at night. It was 20 miles from the town of Staubing on the Danube which had a cinema the POWs were sometimes allowed to visit. On 30 May 1944, Walker and two others, against the general wish of other 'holidaying' prisoners, escaped from the camp. His companions were caught almost instantly, but Walker made it to Staubing. He was recaptured there the next morning while trying to catch a train to Innsbruck. 'The German authorities quickly sent us back to our camps after we had decided to disturb the peace,' he writes, 'we were glad to go, the camp could continue without

us and the inmates could co-operate with the Germans without interference from "tiresome individuals."'

8   The 'Irish Camp' was Stalag III-A at Luckenwalde, 46 miles south of Berlin. Like other 'holiday' or 'rest camps', it was a propaganda camp at which efforts were made, largely unsuccessfully, to recruit Allied POWs in the British Free Corps (BFC) to fight alongside the Germans. Irish POWs were thought by the Germans to be especially susceptible as they had a common enemy in the British and German policy was, should it win the war, for Ireland to be re-unified. Throughout the Second World War, the Irish parliament sustained a policy of neutrality. In Ireland, this period is known as 'the Emergency'. The name comes from the Emergency Powers Act 1939 which was in force from 2 September 1939 for the duration of the war. It lapsed on 2 September 1946 but the state of emergency was not rescinded until 1 September 1976.

9   About 350 yards away from Oflag XII-B, and clearly visible from the camp, was the Hadamar Euthanasia Centre, a death camp for disabled, elderly and mentally ill people whom the Nazis deemed 'unworthy of life'. Between September 1939 and August 1941, over 10,000 men, women and children were gassed at the Euthanasia Centre and their bodies were burnt there. From late 1941 until 1945, a further 4,000 people were killed by lethal injection and deliberate neglect and buried in uniform lines of unmarked graves behind the Centre. Oflag XII-B overlooked Hadamar Station. In his book *My Father's Son: The Memoirs of Major The Earl Haig* (Yorkshire, Leo Cooper, 2000), Haig writes that once a month a 'special' train came in, packed with old and disabled people who were led up the hill to the Centre but that no train ever left with departing patients. He also says that prisoners saw coffins being taken every day to the graves behind the trees. In October 1945, Alfons Klein, the Centre's administrator and six others were tried for war crimes before the United Nations War Crimes Commission in Wiesbaden and found guilty. Three were hung and the rest were given long prison sentences.

15. The Eternal Question

1   British POWs' nickname for Spangenberg.

2   Forces slang, especially used by the RAF, for 'fed up, bored, angry, exasperated'.

3   With the arrival of General Fortune at Oflag XII-B, prisoners were stopped from wearing individualistic clothing and told to dress properly. Haig remembers in *My Father's Son: The Memoirs of Major The Earl Haig*

(Yorkshire, Leo Cooper, 2000) that they had to polish their boots and wear army caps 'in order to impress the Germans and to improve our morale.'

4   6 June 1944 was 'D-Day' for Operation Overlord, the Allies' campaign to liberate Western Europe. The largest armada the world had ever seen of 5,000 ships landed on the beaches of Normandy in France, supported by almost 12,000 aircraft. More than 4,400 Allied forces were killed in the process and many thousands more were wounded. However, more than 100,000 Allied troops marched on into Europe to begin the inevitable defeat of Hitler.

5   In 'They Sent Me to a Rest Camp' in *Detour* (London, The Falcon Press, 1946), Lt Walker describes the capture of his fellow escapees: "The other two were going together and both followed me over [the verandah] loaded with heavy packs on their backs, for they were proceeding on foot and not off to catch a train like myself. Unfortunately, the last one over, in his excitement let go of the rope half way down and fell with a clatter to the ground, this arousing the Germans and spraining his ankle into the bargain.'

6   Oflag X-B Nienburg am. Weser was for French POWs, 35 miles from Hanover, adjacent to Stalag X-C.

7   A straw mattress or under mattress.

8   Operation Valkyrie was a mission to assassinate Hitler and the initial part of a conspiracy by some senior Nazis, including the leaders of the Military Intelligence, to seize power. It took place at one of Hitler's top secret, highly-guarded headquarters, the 'Wolf Lair' (*Wolfsshanze* in German) hidden in woods near Rastenburg, in East Prussia, now Ketrzyn in Poland. On 20 July 1944, Colonel von Stauffenberg, Chief of the Reserve Army, attended a conference there and placed a briefcase containing a bomb under a table and left. At 12:42 pm the bomb exploded, wrecking the shelter. Hitler survived the blast with an injured right arm. Four others present later died. Von Stauffenberg was captured that day and executed early the next morning. The Gestapo arrested at least 7,000 others thought to be involved in the failed coup and executed 5,000 of them. Hitler hung the leaders from meat-hooks with piano wire and filmed their slow deaths to watch later at his own convenience.

9   Heinrich Luitpold Himmler was one of the most powerful men in Nazi Germany. He was the head of the *SchutzStaffel* (SS), a major paramilitary organisation, and the Chief of Police and all security forces, including the Gestapo. Himmler was one of those most directly responsible for the Holocaust. He coordinated the killing of 6 million Jews, between 200,000

and 500,000 Roma, and probably up to another 4 million others, including Poles, Russians, POWs and other groups whom the Nazis deemed unworthy to live such as homosexuals and those with physical and mental disabilities. On 23 May 1945, attempting to flee Germany in disguise, he was captured by British forces. Before he could be questioned, Himmler bit on a cyanide capsule hidden in his mouth and was dead within a few minutes.

10 A grain is a unit of measurement of 64.79891 milligrams, based on the weight of a single grain of barley.

11 Meagre rations.

12 *Don Quixote* by Miguel de Cervantes. Published in two volumes, in 1605 and 1615, it is considered one of the finest literary works ever written and tells of the adventures of Alonso Quijano and his man servant, Sancho Panza.

13 Oflag VIII-F was in a former Benedictine abbey at Wahlett until July 1942 when a new camp at Mährisch-Trübau, now Moravská Třebová in the Czech Republic, became Oflag VIII-F. It held around 2,000 officers, mostly British captured in North Africa and the Greek Islands, but it also held also Greek, French and American POWs. In April 1944, the camp was closed and the prisoners were transferred to other camps.

14 Marlag und Milag Nord was a POW complex for the navy and merchant navy situated at Westertimke, 20 miles northwest of Bremen. It was made up of seven lagers or camps. Lager II, Marlag was for Navy POWs and divided into Marlag O and Marlag M for officers and ratings respectively.

15 Those being repatriated.

16 Brigadier Keith Lindsay Stewart, KBE, CB, DSO, MC (Greek), Legion of Merit (USA), of the New Zealand Expeditionary Forces, served in Crete. He was invalided home but returned to active service in 1943 to command the 5th New Zealand Infantry Brigade in Italy.

17 In his piece for *Detour* (London, The Falcon Press, 1946), Walker writes of Schloss Steinburg, the 'love' or 'holiday' propaganda camp in Bavaria: 'There were girls about in the neighbourhood and came very near the camp. Of course, after four years of captivity the effect of female proximity on love-starved prisoners was not small. Several naval boys were infatuated but had little chance of approaching the object of their affections.' The punishment for prisoners having sexual contacts with women of 'the master race' were severe: a short period of solitary confinement for conversing; a sentence of nine or more months for kissing; and for sexual intercourse, execution.

18 Parrington and Casdagli were in Oflag X-C, Lübeck, in 1941.

19 Brigadier George Herbert Clifton was a determined escaper whose many honours included the DSO with two Bars and the Military Cross.

20 An extract from the *Public Record Office WO 373/100*, London states 'As assistant security officer at OFLAG IX-A/H and a member of the escape committee at OFLAG XII-B (HADAMAR), Major CASDAGLI helped in the maintenance of escape morale. At the same time he sent valuable information to the War Office by secret means.'

16. Portrait of a Prisoner

1 An American heavy bomber used by every branch of the American armed forces during the Second World War and by several Allied forces. It was more modern, faster and had a greater range and heavier bomb load than the Flying Fortress but also had a tendency to catch fire due to the placement of its fuel tanks in the upper fuselage and its lightweight construction.

2 These 'gnats' were De Havilland DH-98 Mosquitoes. They were, small, light, twin-engined two-seat bombers able to carry a 4,000 lb bomb load and to operate by day or night. With flying speeds of over 400 miles per hour, the Mosquitoes were hard to hit. In the Second World War, they were used: as path-finders; to bomb specific targets ahead of Bomber Command; to accompany Bomber Command; and for photo reconnaissance. Fitted with rockets, they attacked ships and, when equipped with radar, it was Britain's most effective night-fighting planes. Almost 8,000 Mosquitoes were manufactured and used by the RAF as reconnaissance planes until 1955.

3 Colonel and Commander.

4 The Hague Conventions of 1899 and 1907 were drawn up at two international conferences at the Hague, Holland. They are a series of international treaties and declarations stating the laws of war and war crimes in international law and were precursors to the Geneva Conventions.

5 The V-1 flying bomb, or 'Vengeance Weapon' from the German *'Vergeltungswaffe'*, was also nicknamed the Doodlebug or Buzz Bomb. Developed by the Luftwaffe to bring terror bombing to London, the V-1 was a completely new weapon: an unmanned gyro-guided plane carrying a 2,000 lb bomb which exploded on impact, causing maximum damage. Its fuselage was made mainly of steel, and its wings of plywood, its simple jet engine pulsed 50 times per second, creating its characteristic buzzing

sound. The V-1 was first fired on London on 13 June 1944. By March 1945, almost 2,500 V-1s had exploded in the city, causing over 6,000 deaths, about 2,000 serious injuries, and destroying thousands of buildings and homes. The V-1 was the forerunner of all rockets, including cruise missiles, and the first known man-made artefact to go into outer space.

6   Schloss Steinburg, the 'love' or 'holiday' propaganda camp in Bavaria, see endnotes 7 and 17 of chapters 14 and 15 respectively.

7   Capt. St. John Aldrich Micklethwait DSO and two Bars was in command of HMS *Sikh* when it was sunk off Tobruk on 14 September 1942; he and most of his crew were taken prisoner. After the war, he returned to the Royal Navy and retired in 1953 as a Rear Admiral.

8   Gerald 'Smash' Kilkelly was the Commanding Officer at the Battle of Gazala in June 1942, at which his unit was wiped out and he was taken prisoner. He was killed by an American shell on 28 August 1944 at Oflag VIII-F.

9   Senior Group Leader.

10   A French expression for hypochondriacs. In this case, it may refer to those who malinger or feign illness especially in order to escape military duties.

11   The second epilogue of Leo Tolstoi's *War and Peace* (Russia, The Russian Messenger, 1869) reflects on the tension between free will and power in relation to the science and laws of history. It argues that the power of the military is not properly understood and, in reality, the more actions a person performs in the military, the less power they will command.

12   Lt General Newman had been made the SBO of all POWs in Germany after General Fortune suffered a stroke affecting his right side on 25 September 1944.

13   George Alexander Eugene Douglas Haig, known as Dawyck, was 26 years old when he painted his portrait of Casdagli and had not yet been to art school. In his book *My Father's Son: The Memoirs of Major The Earl Haig* (Yorkshire, Leo Cooper, 2000), Dawyck says: 'Many officers sat for me and I was able to paint them in oils which had been supplied by the Red Cross.' His father was Field Marshall Earl Haig, who had been in command at the Battle of the Somme in the First World War. In that battle, 600,000 of his men lost their lives. After that war, in 1921, Field Marshall Earl Haig founded the British Legion, which sells poppies to raise money for war-injured soldiers on Armistice Day, also called Remembrance or Poppy Day. Because of his father, Dawyck was moved from Hadamar to Oflag IV-C,

Colditz to join a small group of other *prominente* or 'celebrity' prisoners. These sons of well-known men were singled out as potential hostages on the orders of Hitler and, as a result, lived under continuous threat of execution. After the war, Dawyck studied Fine Art at the Camberwell School of Arts and Crafts in London before becoming a professional painter and running the family estate of Bermersyde in the Scottish Borders.

17. Put Me in the Cooler

1   In their report for the ICRC of their visit to Oflag XII-B on 29 January 1945, Delegates Kleiner and Coctrix state that General Fortune's right side 'has been paralysed for some time. Now his health is improving, but his recovery is slow, with the British doctor fearing he would have a second attack. During the briefing, the German medical staff informed the Delegates that the general had been designated for the next repatriation. His personal servant, Pte MacAllister [sic] William, No. 1270, (twelve years in his service) was also declared unfit for service and will accompany him. It was indicated that General Fortune would leave as soon as possible before he has a relapse.'

2   The V-2, or 'Vengeance Weapon 2' from the German '*Vergeltungswaffe*', like the V-1, was a long-range ballistic missile or rocket targeted on London. See endnote 6, chapter 16.

3   The motorway.

4   The intended target of the bombing was Diez railway station a few miles away. However, flares dropped by pathfinder aircraft were blown off course in a strong wind and some fell into Stalag XII-A. RAF Mosquitoes therefore bombed the wrong target, the highlighted concrete building of the medical block of the Stalag, housing mostly medical personnel. Stalag XII-A was predominantly a transit camp. At this time, it is believed, it was holding over 20,000 POWs, including 3,000 American POWs. Conditions at Stalag XII-A were notoriously abysmal: extreme overcrowding in mainly tented accommodation; starvation rations; no lighting; disease and insanitary conditions; and no recreational facilities at all.

5   63 POWs, mostly American, were killed in the British raid on Stalag XII-A on 23 December 1944.

6   The transit camp was in Hadamar and for officers, not to be confused with the predominately transit camp of Stalag XII-A in Limburg.

7   The Battle of Arnhem took place in Holland between 17 and 26 September

1944. It was part of Operation Market-Garden, a plan by the Allies to bring the war to an early end by parachuting 35,000 troops into Holland to secure six bridges leading to Germany. It was the biggest airborne attack in history and one of the most disastrous. Two American airborne divisions of parachutists, along with the British 1st Airborne Division, were dropped near Arnhem. Due to bad weather, luck, planning and unexpectedly fierce German resistance, they were decimated. Of the British 1st Airborne Division alone, 1,485 were killed or died of their wounds, over 6,500 were captured or missing and only 3,910 returned home safely. Although Operation Market-Garden was a logistical disaster, the fighting of the troops themselves is considered an outstanding example of courage and endurance and one of the greatest feats of arms of the Second World War. In 1977, a film about the battle was made based on Cornelius Ryan's book of the same name, *A Bridge Too Far*. Directed by Richard Attenborough, its star cast included Dirk Bogarde, Michael Caine, Sean Connery and Laurence Olivier.

18. The Flap is On

1   In December 1944, fighting tore apart the Greek capital of Athens; the events of that time became known as the Dekemvriana or Δεκεμβριανά in Greek. The Germans had retreated from Greece in October that year, and on 18 October, British troops entered Athens and the long Occupation of the city was over. Six days later, the Greek government-in-exile led by the prominent liberal, Georgos Papandreou, returned to Greece. All of the Greek resistance forces were put under the command of a British officer, General Scobie who demanded that the left-wing group, EAM (*Εθνικό Απελευθερωτικό Μέτωπο*, National Liberation Front) demobilise its guerrilla army, ELAS (*Ελληνική Λαϊκός Απελευθερωτικός Στρατός*, Greek Popular Liberation Army), but did not ask the same of EAM's great enemy, the right-wing group EDES (*Εθνικός Δημοκρατικός Ελληνικός Σύνδεσμος*, National Republican Greek League) which was backed by the British. On 3 December 1944, EAM organised a demonstration in Athens against the order. As the peaceful demonstration of 250,000 approached the Tomb of the Unknown Soldier in Syntagma, the central square of Athens, they were shot at from roofs of the Grande Bretagne Hotel and several other buildings, as well as by policemen in the crowd; 28 demonstrators were killed and 148 wounded. Fierce fighting broke out for the rest of the month between EAM and EDES. On 15 January 1945, General Scobie accepted a request for a ceasefire from EAM.

2   The American fighter aircraft Lockheed P-38 Lightning had twin booms and

a cockpit in the central casing of the plane. It was a long-range escort fighter with drop tanks under its wings used for dive bombing, ground attack and night fighting.

3   Anti-aircraft fire.

4   General Fortune refused repatriation, which was offered both on health grounds and for his daughter's wedding, saying: 'I brought the men out, I'll come back with them.' General Fortune was liberated from Limburg Hospital by a US First Army tank column. The story is told by war correspondent James McDowall in the *Aberdeen Journal*, March 28, 1945. McDowall writes: 'When the Americans entered it (the hospital) he was walking about with the aid of a cane, dressed in battledress, and already in command of the establishment.' His batman, Private McAllister, who had served with him for twelve years, was still at his side and went home with him where he stayed. General Fortune was knighted by King George on 19 April 1945 in recognition of valuable services to British POWs in Germany. Among other honours, on 23 July 1948, he was awarded Grand Officer of the Royal Order of the Phoenix by the King of the Hellenes in recognition of distinguished services to the Allies and the Greek people. Major-General Sir Victor Morven Fortune KBE, CB, DSO died at home on 2 January 1949, aged 65; he is buried in Auchencairn Cemetery, next to his wife, Eleanor.

5   That night, Brigadier Clifton took advantage of an air attack and the camp's move to escape. When it was dark, he simply slipped through the perimeter wire without anyone noticing. For four days and three nights, he walked through a 'death zone' where, as an escaping POW, he would have been shot on sight had he been discovered. He walked over 100 miles until he was just behind the German lines near Weis. He hid until the enemy retreated during the night and reported to an American unit the next morning.

6   Oflag XII-B is now Limburger Domsingknaben, a boarding school for choirboys. The Hadamar Euthanasia Centre is now a psychiatric hospital and also houses a museum.

LIBERATION
19. The Americans are Coming!

1   'Heavies' were long-range heavy bombers, such as the British Avro Lancaster and the American Flying Fortress, otherwise known as the Boeing B-17 and the Consolidated B-24 Liberator, respectively.

2   The American Republic P-47 Thunderbolt were one of the main American

fighter bombers of the Second World War. Heavily armed with four machine guns per wing, they could carry five-inch rockets or a bomb load of 2,500lbs.

3   The action of firing several guns at the same time.

4   The 7th Armoured Division of the 1st American Army was nicknamed the 'Lucky Seventh' because of its disproportionately high success rate in taking enemy vehicles and prisoners.

5   Shermans were M4 General Shermans tanks, designed and built by the United States. A total of 49,324 Sherman tanks were produced in 11 plants between 1942 and 1946 and were deployed by both the Americans and the Allies.

6   Dulag-Luft Wetzlar, 45 miles due north of Frankfurt, was mainly a transit camp for Air Force POWs but it had also been an interrogation centre. It had a reputation for extorting information under torture and offering bleak acts of sexual perversion in exchange for information.

20. My Cup of Happiness

1   The Douglas C-47 Skytrain or Dakota was used extensively by the Allies for transporting troops, wounded personnel and cargo.

2   The Siegfried Line was a defence system stretching more than 390 miles between the borders of Holland and Switzerland. Constructed of over 18,000 bunkers, tank traps and tunnels, it was built by Hitler between 1938 and 1940 for propaganda rather than any military purpose.

3   The village of Oakley Green was two and a half miles away from Windsor Castle. In Oakley Green was Tall Trees, the home of the Hon. Mrs Mary Morgan-Jones and her husband, Lt Col. Gwyn Morgan-Jones at which Joyce and Tony, Casdagli's wife and son, had been living for over a year and where Casdagli was to join them.

4   Perhaps Abington aerodrome which was used extensively by the RAF throughout the war, but it lies south, not east, of Oxford. However, the distance between Abingdon and Reception Camp 90, Chalfont St Giles, is 44 miles which would fit in with the timing the journey took.

5   Ludgrove School was Tony's 'prep school', a boarding school for boys up to the age of thirteen. It was twelve and a half miles away from Tall Trees.

BIBLIOGRAPHY

Adams, Guy, (ed.) *Backwater Oflag IX A/H Lower Camp* (London, Frederick Muller Ltd, 1944).

Beckwith, E.G.C., (ed.) *The Quill: A Collection of Prose, Verse and Sketches by Officers Prisoner-of-War in Germany, 1940 – 1945* (London, Country Life Ltd., 1947).

Brickhill, Paul, *Reach for the Sky: The Story of Douglas Bader DSO, DFC* (London, Odhams Press Ltd., 1954).

Casdagli, E.T., *The Man From The White Mountain* (privately published, 1974).

Cervantes, Miguel de, *The Adventures of Don Quixote*, Trans. J. M. Cohen (Middlesex, Penguin Classics, 1950).

Charny, Daniel, (ed.) *The Power of Making: The importance of being skilled* (London, V&A Publishing, 2011).

Crawley, Aidan, *Escape from Germany* (London, HMSO, 1985).

Foot M.R.D. and Langley, J.M., *MI9: Escape and Evasion 1939 – 1945* (London, Book Club Associates, 1979).

Green, Peter, *The March East 1945: The Final Days of Oflag IX A/H and A/Z* (Stroud, Spellmount, 2012).

Haig, The Earl, *My Father's Son: The Memoirs of Major The Earl Haig* (Yorkshire, Leo Cooper, 2000).

Hamson, C.J., *Liber in Vinculis or The Mock Turtle's Adventure: written in captivity 1941 – 1945* (Cambridge, Trinity College, 1989).

Harling, Robert, (ed.) *House & Garden Book of Cottages* (Condé Nast V Publications, 1963).

Hildyard, Myles, *It Is Bliss Here: Letters Home 1939 – 1945* (London, Bloomsbury Publishing, 2005).

Homer, *The Iliad*, Trans. E.V. Rieu (Middlesex, Penguin Classics, 1950).

Kee, Robert, *A Crowd is Not Company* (Great Britain, Eyre & Spottiswoode Ltd, 1947).

MacKenzie, S.P., *The Colditz Myth: British and Commonwealth Prisoners of War in Nazi Germany* (Oxford, Oxford University Press, 2004).

MacLean, Alistair, *The Guns of Naverone* (United Kingdom, Collins, 1957).

Lawrence T.E., *Revolt in the Desert* (London, Jonathan Cape, 1927).

Neave, Airey, *Saturday at MI9* (Great Britain, Hodder & Stoughton Ltd., 1969).

Neave, Airey, *The Flames of Calais: A Soldier's Battle 1940* (Great Britain, Hodder & Stoughton Ltd., 1972).

Newark, Tim, *The Fighting Irish: The Story of the Extraordinary Irish Soldier* (London, Constable & Robinson Ltd., 2012).

Nicholls, Dominie, *Quite A Lot: A Memoir by Dominie Nicholls* (privately published, 1984).

Poole, Jack, *Undiscovered Ends* (London, Cassell & Company Ltd, 1957).

Powell, Dilys, *The Villa Ariadne* (Great Britain, Hodder & Stoughton Ltd., 1973).

Ryan, Cornelius, *A Bridge Too Far* (United States of America, Simon & Schuster, 1974)

Rolf, David, *Prisoners of the Reich: Germany's Captives 1939 – 1945* (Great Britain, Leo Cooper Ltd., 1988).

Shanahan, Kirsty, (ed.) *Harrow Record: News and Views from Harrow School* (Spring 2012).

Tolstoy, Leo, *War and Peace* (Hertfordshire, Wordsworth Classics, 1993).

Vere Benson, S., *The Observer Book of Birds* (London, Frederick Warne and Co. Ltd., 1960).

Watson, Victor, *The Waddingtons Story: From the Early Days to Monopoly, the Maxwell Bids and into the Next Millennium* (Jeremy Mills Publishing, 2008).

Wilde, Oscar, *The Ballad of Reading Gaol* (Leonard Smithers, 1898).

Wood, J.E.R., (ed.) *Detour: The Story of Oflag IVC* (London, The Falcon Press, 1946).

Wylie, Neville, *Barbed Wire Diplomacy: Britain, Germany, and the Politics of Prisoners of War, 1939 – 1945* (Oxford, Oxford University Press, 2010).

Zervos, Stella Reader, *One Woman's War: A Diary of an English Woman living in Occupied Greece 1939 – 1945* (Athens, Athens Centre Academic Press, 1991).

ABBREVIATIONS

AA	Anti-aircraft artillery
ADC	Aide-de-Camp
AIF	Australian Imperial Force
AQMG	Assistant Quartermaster-General
ARP	Air Raid Precautions
ATS	Auxiliary Territorial Service
BFC	British Free Corps
BMM	British Military Mission
Brig.	Brigadier
Capt.	Captain
CB	Companion of the Order of the Bath
CCA	Combat Command A
CIRC	Committee of the International Red Cross
Col.	Colonel
CMF	Central Mediterranean Force
DADOS	Deputy Assistant Director of Ordnance to Services
DFC	Distinguished Flying Cross
DSO	Distinguished Service Order
Dulag Luft	Durchgangslager der Luftwaffe (transit camp Air Force)
EAM	*Εθνικό Απελευθερωτικό Μέτωπο* (National Liberation Front)
EDES	*Εθνικός Δημοκρατικός Ελληνικός Σύνδεσμος* (National Republican Greek League)
ELAS	*Ελληνική Λαϊκός Απελευθερωτικός Στρατός* (Greek Popular Liberation Army)
F/Lt	Flight Lieutenant
F/O	Flying Officer
FO	Foreign Office
Gen.	General
Gen. List	General List of General Service Corps of British Army
GOC	General Officer Commanding
GSC	General Service Corps
HMAS	His Majesty's Australian Ship
HMS	His Majesty's Ship
HMSO	Her Majesty's Stationery Office

HMT	His Majesty's Troopship
Hon.	The Honourable
HQ	Head Quarters
ICRC	International Committee of the Red Cross
Ilag	Internment camp for Allied civilians
IWM	Imperial War Museum
Ju-52	Junkers aircraft
KBE	Knight Commander of the Most Excellent Order of the British Empire
Lt	Lieutenant
Lt Col.	Lieutenant Colonel
Lt Gen.	Lieutenant General
Maj.	Major
Maj. Gen.	Major General
MC	Military Cross
MI	Military Intelligence
MI	Medical Inspection
MI9	Military Intelligence 9 escape and evasion (British)
MIS-X	Military Intelligence Section escape and evasion (USA)
MO	Medical Officer
MP	Member of Parliament
Marlag	*Marinelager* (Navy camp)
NCO	Non-Commissioned Officer
NKVD	*Narodnyy Komissariat Vnutrennikh Del* (People's Commissariat for Internal Affairs)
NZ	New Zealand
NZEF	New Zealand Expeditionary Force
OBE	Order of the British Empire
OCCWC	Office of the Chief Counsel for War Crimes
Oflag	*Offizierslager* (officers' POW camp)
OKW	*Oberkommando der Wehrmacht* (Supreme Command of the Armed Forces)
OR	Other Ranks
P/O	Pilot Officer
PMC	President of the Mess Committee
POW	Prisoner of war
QC	Queen's Counsel
RA	Royal Artillery
RADC	Royal Army Dental Corps

RAF	Royal Air Force
RAMC	Royal Army Medical Corps
RAOC	Royal Army Ordnance Corps
RASC	Royal Army Service Corps
RC	Regional Command
RC	Roman Catholic
RE	Royal Engineers
RM	Royal Marines
RN	Royal Navy
RTR	Royal Tank Regiment
SAO	Senior Allied Officer
SBO	Senior British Officer
Sgt	Sergeant
SOE	Special Operations Executive
Sqn Ldr	Squadron Leader
SS	*Schutzstaffeln* (protection squad)
Stalag	*Stammlager* (fixed POW camp for OR)
Stalag Luft	POW camp for Allied airmen
TAB	Typhoid paratyphoid A and B vaccine
TB	Tuberculosis
USA	United States of America
USAAC	United States Army Air Corps
V-1, V-2	*Vergeltungswaffe* (vengeance weapon 1 & 2)
WAAF	Women's Auxiliary Air Force
WO	War Office (British)
YMCA	Young Men's Christian Association

INDEX

Names and Places
(excluding Endnotes)

MANY THANKS

Alexis Penny Casdagli would like to thank Gwen Williamson, Chris R. McDermott, Phil Irish, Alyson Hurst of G. F Smith, Rob Squires of the Pureprint Group, Dave West of Studio 22, Theodora Philippidou, Jen Green, Manju Manglani, Claire Buonaquisti and Frances Hetherington for all their work and generous support in the making of this book, without whom it would not have been possible.

Many others have helped too in different ways and my thanks are due to Cornelia Albert at the Swiss Ministry of Defence; Alex Bacopoulos; Lynda Bellingham OBE; Fabrizio Benzi, Marie-Laure Cap and Karen Terzi-Tanaka at the International Committee of the Red Cross, Geneva; Don, Margaret and Alexis Bergomi; Anthony Casdagli CBE; Christopher Casdagli; Daphne Casdagli; David Casdagli; Valissa Casdagli; Kaia Charles at the Victoria and Albert Museum; Ruth Denli at Harrow School Outfitters; Anastassis Fafalios; Emily Friedlander; Kristen Harrison; Iro Green; Peter Green; Nichola Jones of the British Red Cross; Stelios Korvas; Christos Laskaris; Jemma Lee, Archivist at the British Red Cross; Christopher Long; Andrew Macdonald at the Imperial War Museum; Angharad Meredith, Archivist and Records Manager, Harrow School; Andrew Mussell, Archivist at the Honourable Society of Grays Inn; Ilias Nanas; Luka Niedermeier; Simon Offord, Archvist at the Imperial War Museum; Akrivi Papadaki; Victoria Prescott; Sara Alexandra Rocha; John Ross (the younger); Graeme Rayner at Hain Daniels; James Scott; Perena Shryane and James Virgin of the Harrow Association; Jenny Simmons, Communication Manager at Harrow School; Jon Smith, Archivist at the Wren Library, Trinity College Cambridge; Elias Staris; Valerie Youmans; Yannis Zerbos.